SOCIAL ISSUES
FIRSTHAND

| Child Abuse and Neglect

Other Books in the Social Issues Firsthand Series:

AIDS

Body Piercing and Tattoos

Cults

Date and Acquaintance Rape

Drunk Driving

Eating Disorders

Gangs

Prostitution

Sexual Predators

Teenage Pregnancy

Welfare

Child Abuse and Neglect

Stefan Kiesbye, Book Editor

GREENHAVEN PRESS
A part of Gale, Cengage Learning

Detroit • New York • San Francisco • New Haven, Conn • Waterville, Maine • London

GALE
CENGAGE Learning™

Christine Nasso, *Publisher*
Elizabeth Des Chenes, *Managing Editor*

© 2008 Greenhaven Press, a part of Gale, Cengage Learning

For more information, contact:
Greenhaven Press
27500 Drake Rd.
Farmington Hills, MI 48331-3535
Or you can visit our Internet site at gale.cengage.com.

For product information and technology assistance, contact us at

Gale Customer Support, 1-800-877-4253
For permission to use material from this text or product, submit all requests online at www.cengage.com/permissions

Further permissions questions can be emailed to permissionrequest@cengage.com

Articles in Greenhaven Press anthologies are often edited for length to meet page requirements. In addition, original titles of these works are changed to clearly present the main thesis and to explicitly indicate the author's opinion. Every effort is made to ensure that Greenhaven Press accurately reflects the original intent of the authors. Every effort has been made to trace the owners of copyrighted material.

Cover photograph copyright Mandy Godbehear, 2008. Used under license from Shutterstock.com.

ISBN-13: 978-0-7377-4272-5 (hardcover)
ISBN-10: 0-7377-4272-0 (hardcover)

Library of Congress Control Number: 2008924438

Printed in the United States of America
1 2 3 4 5 6 7 12 11 10 09 08

Contents

Foreword   7

Introduction   10

Chapter 1: Abuse by Family and Caretakers

1. Abuse by Family Friends   14

   Sophie, as told to Megan Bayliss

   Assaulted repeatedly by men, a woman struggles with alcohol and drugs before starting to get back on her feet.

2. A Violent Father   18

   Jenie Pak

   A daughter recalls the fragile, disturbed relationship with her father.

Chapter 2: Boys and Abuse

1. Verbal and Physical Abuse   26

   Jim Van Buskirk

   Growing up in an abusive family, a gay teenager becomes the target of his mother's scorn and his father's beatings.

2. Father-Son Incest   40

   Jimmy, as told to Michel Dorais

   A son craving his father's love endures sexual abuse and spirals into drug use and self-destructive behavior.

3. Abused by a Priest   47

   John Salveson

   After years of being stalked, molested, and manipulated, a survivor exposes past wrongdoings and battles the church publicly to break the silence surrounding clerical abuse.

4. Grandfather Tormented Us   61

   Mike, as told to Kim Etherington

   After being sexually abused by his grandfather as a child, a man confronts his abuser. He and his brother must come to terms with their conflicting feelings of love and disgust.

5. An Abusive Mother   69
   Fred Mimmack
   A successful therapist and scholar struggles to find him-
   self after growing up with an abusive mother.

Chapter 3: The Perpetrators of Abuse

1. A Victim Works with Sex Offenders   76
   Pamela D. Schultz
   Being a survivor of child sexual abuse, a female therapist
   decides to work with male perpetrators to gain insight
   into the making of a sex offender and achieves a measure
   of peace.

2. A Cycle of Abuse   86
   Billy, as told to Pamela D. Schultz
   Having been abused early on in his life, a convicted child
   molester describes his path toward violence and how he's
   attempting to reenter society.

Organizations to Contact   103

For Further Research   107

Index   111

Foreword

Social issues are often viewed in abstract terms. Pressing challenges such as poverty, homelessness, and addiction are viewed as problems to be defined and solved. Politicians, social scientists, and other experts engage in debates about the extent of the problems, their causes, and how best to remedy them. Often overlooked in these discussions is the human dimension of the issue. Behind every policy debate over poverty, homelessness, and substance abuse, for example, are real people struggling to make ends meet, to survive life on the streets, and to overcome addiction to drugs and alcohol. Their stories are ubiquitous and compelling. They are the stories of everyday people—perhaps your own family members or friends—and yet they rarely influence the debates taking place in state capitols, the national Congress, or the courts.

The disparity between the public debate and private experience of social issues is well illustrated by looking at the topic of poverty. Each year the U.S. Census Bureau establishes a poverty threshold. A household with an income below the threshold is defined as poor, while a household with an income above the threshold is considered able to live on a basic subsistence level. For example, in 2003 a family of two was considered poor if its income was less than $12,015; a family of four was defined as poor if its income was less than $18,810. Based on this system, the bureau estimates that 35.9 million Americans (12.5 percent of the population) lived below the poverty line in 2003, including 12.9 million children below the age of eighteen.

Commentators disagree about what these statistics mean. Social activists insist that the huge number of officially poor Americans translates into human suffering. Even many families that have incomes above the threshold, they maintain, are likely to be struggling to get by. Other commentators insist that the statistics exaggerate the problem of poverty in the United States. Compared to people in developing countries, they point out, most so-called poor families have a high quality of life. As stated by journalist Fidelis Iyebote, "Cars are owned by 70 percent of 'poor' households. . . . Color televisions belong to 97 percent of the 'poor' [and] videocassette recorders belong to nearly 75 percent. . . . Sixty-four percent have microwave ovens, half own a stereo system, and over a quarter possess an automatic dishwasher."

However, this debate over the poverty threshold and what it means is likely irrelevant to a person living in poverty. Simply put, poor people do not need the government to tell them whether they are poor. They can see it in the stack of bills they cannot pay. They are aware of it when they are forced to choose between paying rent or buying food for their children. They become painfully conscious of it when they lose their homes and are forced to live in their cars or on the streets. Indeed, the written stories of poor people define the meaning of poverty more vividly than a government bureaucracy could ever hope to. Narratives composed by the poor describe losing jobs due to injury or mental illness, depict horrific tales of childhood abuse and spousal violence, recount the loss of friends and family members. They evoke the slipping away of social supports and government assistance, the descent into substance abuse and addiction, the harsh realities of life on the streets. These are the perspectives on poverty that are too often omitted from discussions over the extent of the problem and how to solve it.

Greenhaven Press's Social Issues Firsthand series provides a forum for the often-overlooked human perspectives on society's most divisive topics of debate. Each volume focuses on one social issue and presents a collection of ten to sixteen narratives by those who have had personal involvement with the topic. Extra care has been taken to include a diverse range of perspectives. For example, in the volume on adoption, readers will find the stories of birth parents who have made an adoption plan, adoptive parents, and adoptees themselves. After exposure to these varied points of view, the reader will have a clearer understanding that adoption is an intense, emotional experience full of joyous highs and painful lows for all concerned.

The debate surrounding embryonic stem cell research illustrates the moral and ethical pressure that the public brings to bear on the scientific community. However, while nonexperts often criticize scientists for not considering the potential negative impact of their work, ironically the public's reaction against such discoveries can produce harmful results as well. For example, although the outcry against embryonic stem cell research in the United States has resulted in fewer embryos being destroyed, those with Parkinson's, such as actor Michael J. Fox, have argued that prohibiting the development of new stem cell lines ultimately will prevent a timely cure for the disease that is killing Fox and thousands of others.

Each book in the series contains several features that enhance its usefulness, including an in-depth introduction, an annotated table of contents, bibliographies for further research, a list of organizations to contact, and a thorough index. These elements—combined with the poignant voices of people touched by tragedy and triumph—make the Social Issues Firsthand series a valuable resource for research on today's topics of political discussion.

Introduction

It is too often the same story. Parents cross the line, relatives become criminals, and children suffer without being able to confide in anyone. Too many victims of abuse choose silence because the consequences of telling the truth seem insurmountable. How does a seven-year-old tell his teacher that she's being abused at home? How does a child tell her father that his brother is molesting her? Instead of talking about the abuse, children blame themselves, internalize that the abuse was really their fault, or that physical abuse was only a sign of parental love. When confronted by their victims, too many molesters blame the innocent, and the victims believe them.

The U.S. Department of Health and Human Services (HHS) found that "more than 60 percent of child victims were neglected by their parents or other caregivers. About 18 percent were physically abused, 10 percent were sexually abused, and 7 percent were emotionally maltreated. In addition, 15 percent were associated with 'other' types of maltreatment based on specific State laws and policies. A child could be a victim of more than one type of maltreatment."

According to the HHS, 78.4 percent of the perpetrators of child abuse and neglect are the victim's parents. Despite public awareness, child abuse is still a problem within families. Other relatives account for 6.4 percent, and unmarried partners of a parent for another 4.1 percent. It is hardly ever a stranger harming the child, or an unidentified intruder molesting or exploiting minors. Many would argue child abuse is not a problem of unsafe streets or strangers with candy; instead the very people who are legally responsible to care and look out for their children perpetrate the crimes.

Today, about 60 million survivors of childhood sexual abuse live in America. While the number is staggering, the long-term consequences of child abuse are possibly more dramatic. The effects on survivors of abuse are fear, anxiety, mental health disorders, poor social skills, inappropriate sexual behavior, low self-confidence, drug and alcohol abuse, and the inability to enter or sustain close relationships. Since personal boundaries have so often been disregarded, it is difficult for survivors to establish a healthy sense of self. The lines between respectful and damaging social interaction, between care and intrusion, can be permanently blurred. The damages to self-esteem and social behavior affect men and women equally. Both male and female victims of abuse show increased suicidal tendencies. Men have a high risk to develop mental illness, while women are in danger of sliding into alcohol abuse and prostitution.

Not only are child abuse victims in danger of harming themselves, they are also more likely to inflict harm on others. A study by the National Institute of Justice (NIJ) shows that individuals who were abused or neglected as children, were 59 percent more likely to be arrested as juveniles than their unharmed counterparts. As adults, the likelihood of arrest was still 28 percent higher than those that grew up without abuse. Violent crimes perpetrated by victims of child abuse were 30 percent higher. The NIJ writes that the study's findings "showed that childhood abuse and neglect increased the odds of future delinquency and adult criminality overall by 29 percent." Thus, child abuse creates a cycle of violence that goes beyond the family and impacts society as a whole.

And the violence does not stop at juvenile delinquency. Child abuse not only limits the survivors' own lives, but can have devastating effects on the lives of the next generation and beyond. Some sexually abused children can only relate to others in purely sexual terms, and they become perpetrators of child abuse themselves, never having learned how to parent appropriately. Parents who experienced child abuse often punish their own children in the ways they were treated. Emotionally abused children are more likely to become emotionally abusive parents. These parents lack the range of emotional and physical responses necessary to deal with the challenges of raising a family. They have never learned the strategies to cope with conflict and fall back on the harmful methods their own parents used. Stress, poverty, and social isolation can increase the risk of abuse.

To break the cycle of abuse, these parents need to grow aware of the ways in which they are treating their children and learn to foster healthy relationships. To help them and their children, early identification of abused and neglected children is of the essence: but it is only a first step. Educational programs are necessary to increase awareness of abuse and its prevention. These can help adults improve the skills needed for successful parenting, and teach personal safety skills to minors. Community support groups and intervention programs promote effective communication and problem solving within the family unit. Crisis assistance and professional counseling and therapy services for survivors can help individuals deal with and overcome the traumatic effects of abuse.

Child abuse is not a comfortable topic of discussion, not for victims and their abusers, not for the ones witnessing abuse, or even society as a whole. Yet the first step to breaking the cycle of violence is to break the cycle of silence. The following viewpoints demonstrate the sensitive nature of child abuse, offer a forum for those affected by child abuse, and provide an environment for further discussion.

Abuse by Family and Caretakers

Abuse by Family Friends

Sophie, as told to Megan Bayliss

Sophie recounts her tumultuous childhood and early adulthood. From a young age, she was abused and raped by a trusted family friend and her father's coworkers or helpers. The traumatic experience led her to start drinking and using drugs. Only after pregnancy did she tell her parents, and telling her story has helped her overcome the horrors of her past. Sophie's real name was changed to protect her identity.

I'm now 38. Can you believe it? I never thought I'd make it this far. Between the ages of seven and 15 there is only a 12 month period where I can't remember being abused. Five different men but all with the same story: I was beautiful, I was special and they loved me. My parents never knew. I could never tell them because I was scared that I'd get into trouble or that I wouldn't be believed. Sometimes the abuse happened in my home, while they were there too but they never suspected because they were busy and they thought the men were their good friends.

The first time it happened I was embarrassed and I didn't say "no" because I wasn't sure if I was allowed to. He had bought me lots of gifts and made a big fuss of me. He was a very important man and was my Dad's biggest boss. He abused me non-stop until I was around 13. I guess I got too big for him then and he didn't like me anymore. Thank God! He got more and more aggressive in his abuse of me as the years went on. Sometimes I fought him but he used to hurt me more so I just gave into it. I *hate* him. He was so sneaky that he'd even come to my school, find out what sport I was playing and turn up at practice and track me down at friends' houses. He was a pedophile.

The second perpetrator was a person who did part-time work for my parents. I know he got to my younger sister too but we never talk about it. I saw him and her in the laundry and I shut my eyes because I was so scared. He used to get me in the kitchen when nobody else was around. I would do what ever I could to not be at home on the days I knew he was coming but sometimes Mum and Dad would get angry at me and tell me I had to be around to tell him where things were. I so wanted to tell them but I just couldn't make the words come out of my mouth. I tried to make them aware that something was wrong by writing swear words all over the path. I thought they'd see the words and want to know how I knew them. That was when I was going to tell them how I knew what a penis was. After I'd found out from my friends how to spell really bad swear words I wrote them everywhere in chalk. But it rained and the words got washed away before my parents got to see them and go ballistic.

The third perpetrator was also a work mate of my father's. It only ever happened once from him and it wasn't too bad. He just felt me all over. He didn't stick anything into me. He was very scared too. He kept looking over his shoulder and if he heard a noise he'd quickly take his hands away from me. When I think about this, I think that he was probably a man who could have been helped. He wasn't sure [of] what he was doing. It was almost as though it was the first time he'd done it. If he did do it again, I hope some other kid was braver than me and told on him so that he could get help before it was too late.

The fourth perpetrator was the worst. It is the most dreadful thing that ever happened to me and I don't really want to talk it. I was raped by four men. I didn't know them. I was walking home and they grabbed me. When I had to continue walking home, people must have known what happened. I was a mess. My clothes were torn, I had blood all over me and my face was swollen from being hit. People looked at me in disgust. They stepped around me. Nobody helped me. I knew my parents wouldn't be home so I fixed myself up and went to bed for a few days. Mum thought I had got my first period and was feeling sick. I told her I got into a fight with my friend to explain the marks on my face. She grounded me for a month because fighting was a dreadful thing to do.

After the [fifth] rape I started drinking and doing drugs. I was trying to stop myself from thinking about everything that had happened to me and trying to build up courage to tell my parents the truth. The man that used to sell me Pot and give me alcohol helped himself to me one day. I fought like a tiger and it stopped him from raping me. But he told lots of stories about me and made me out to look like the worst kid in town.

After I had my first baby I decided to tell my parents what had happened. They *believed me.* I was so happy. They helped me to talk to the police but there was nothing much that could be done. I couldn't remember dates, time of day, rooms it happened in, and all the other million things they asked me. The police were very understanding though.

For all of the sexual abuse that happened, I think I've finally got it together. I am still frightened to be alone and I don't trust men much but I lead a good life and I have met some really good counselors who have helped me sort out everything that has happened. Mum and I often talk about why I couldn't tell them and she says that she always had some suspicions but was also too embarrassed to raise [the issue]. She said she figured that if something was happening that I'd tell her. Funny how we were both thinking similar things but embarrassment and fear stopped us from checking it out.

There's lots of kids out there who are going through the same thing as I went through. I want to give parents the message to *please don't be embarrassed to talk to your kids about this stuff*. Kids don't know how to talk about it and kids really do think they are going to get into trouble. Sexual abuse is rude and kids don't usually talk about rude things with their parents. It's very, very hard to do.

Thank you. That is my short story. Now I feel all shaky and I want to cry but I am glad I've done it. I want to help stop child sexual abuse.

A Violent Father

Jenie Pak

In "Dog Dreams" poet Jenie Pak explores the links between her childhood abuse and her recurrent nightmares. Watching horror movies with her dad, the author learns early on that underneath the surface of everyday life, darkness is always ready to strike. Her essay is an examination of her body language and the many ways in which her body and mind still respond to the fear of sudden beatings by her father. Jenie Pak received her master of fine arts degree in poetry from Cornell University and has poetry or fiction published in Alligator Juniper, Blithe House Quarterly, Five Fingers Review, Love Shook My Heart II, Many Mountains Moving, *and the* Oakland Review.

Friday the Thirteenth. Halloween. Bram Stoker's Dracula, the video camera version on PBS, so real-to-life I had nightmares for three nights in a row. *Sleepaway Camp. Invasion of the Body Snatchers. Prom Night. Dressed to Kill. Carrie.*

Not your A-list of movies to rent from your local video store? Not mine, either. But these were the movies I grew up watching because my father liked them and whatever he watched, I watched. My sister too, who was always too squeamish to bear the gruesome scenes. She would lay her palms flat over her eyes, bring her head down, and demand, *Tell me when it's over. It's over*, I'd say, though it really wasn't. So usually she would catch a glimpse of the ax lowering over the neck, the knife pulling out of the back before the body fell over.

My father also liked Westerns, boxing, action-adventure, and kung fu films. Anything violent, full of car chases, men beating up on each other—the body always running away from itself, colliding fast into another. I watched them all, sitting cross-legged next to him on the carpeted floor. If my sister wanted to go off to a room somewhere by herself and read, my father shouted, *Get over here. You're a part of this family too.*

A Mischievous Father

During commercials, my father would turn his head slyly toward us, eyes glimmering with mischief, and bring his hands up like claws by his chest. He would lunge—a werewolf, a vampire, a crazed killer—then laugh at the shock rushing down our lungs. And then we would laugh too, thinking, what a father, this guy, that we have. Sometimes, after our late-night walks together, he would dare us to walk down the ramp behind our apartment building. It was dark, no lamps or anything, and the ramp was long. We weren't allowed to run, we had to walk slowly down there, feeling our way in the dark for what might be something hairy, like a face with big pointy ears and fangs. If we said no, my father would say things like, *You're so chicken, so scaredy-cat, how will you ever amount to anything in the world? Let's see who is more brave*, he would declare, pitting my sister and me against each other.

I remember spending afternoons with my father in our Queens apartment, stepping on his back, stepping down with one foot, then with the other. *The lower back*, he would command, *step there, and now the legs, step on the calves.* He would turn his opera records up high. *La Traviata*, the album cover of a male statue in full moonlight. Purple flowers illuminated by that natural shimmer. That was my favorite. But there were others. *Carmen, Rigoletto, La Bohème.* He would tell me the stories of these operas. *This woman is singing because her love betrayed her. This woman has just swallowed poison and will die after this song is over. That man loves only one woman but she won't give him the time of day.* Always about love, and de-

19

sire. Always, someone dying, someone lying terminally sick in his musty bed. But I listened willingly. I listened to the sharp soaring voices, thinking there was something else they were trying to tell me if only I listened deep enough.

Beatings and Lectures

I looked up to my father, the well-educated man who had taught history at an all-girls high school in South Korea. There are black-and-white photos of him, young and smiling at the camera, surrounded by his students. You can tell that they all have crushes on him, the ones who got to sit closest to him, smiling the biggest smiles. My father had read all of the classics, [Fyodor] Dostoyevsky, Plato, [Friedrich] Nietzsche, the Bible, and so forth. He had studied religion, philosophy, history, literature, listened to classical music, and wrote poetry standing by his small window on lonely December mornings. So when he punished my sister and me by hitting us with a golf club or a huge brass pole, I didn't think, *This is a man who is angry and in pain.* I didn't think, *This is a man who has lost his mind.*

I joke sometimes that I could never be a waitress since I'm just too clumsy. I see myself spilling plates of hot food on customers, bumping into tables and counters so my hips and arms bruise to small yellowish flowers. And quietly to myself I think, maybe it is because of the beatings I received to the backs of my knees, so I lack balance, so I find myself walking in a sort of daze, losing the feeling in my legs. My sister has a sort of funny walk too. It's hard to explain really, but often it seems like she has a hard time getting to where she needs to go. So I remember those times, my father with the golf club in his hand, swinging the thing like it will give him glorious victory. I remember my mother crying but doing nothing to stop him. I remember most the dreaded lectures he would give us after the beatings. *This is only because I love you so much, this is because you need someone to teach you right from wrong, and as much as I hate it I am the one who has to do this.*

Sometimes I forget, but for instance, when I begin to make friends with someone new, I find myself inevitably telling the story of my father. I find myself saying things like, *He hit me with golf clubs and brass poles kept in the corner of the hall closet. He hit me on the head with the back of his hand so hard my barrettes flew off into the next room.* I wait for this new friend's reaction, wait for a little bit of shock in her eyes or for some shade of sympathy. But mostly, I wait for that change in her, the one lone thing that will suddenly overtake her body, and I will know that I have lost this friend forever. That I have had too unbelievable a childhood, that I would share ugly secrets like this with someone as nice as her. Is this shame? Is this self-pity? Is it simply me saying, *This is me, get to know me for who I am?* And when she pauses for a moment, then says, *Many of my friends tell me stories like these,* or, *My father beat me too,* I feel relief. It wasn't just me and my sister. It wasn't just my father.

The Attacks of 9/11

Today, the world has been turned upside down. The World Trade Center has been destroyed by hijacked planes that crashed into those twin towers. Fire and smoke, firefighters and police officers, pedestrians covered in dust and debris saying things like, *I couldn't see anything, it was dark, there was for a moment this eerie silence.* My ex-girlfriend calls me early this morning in tears. *Something terrible has happened,* she says. *Turn on the news.* I sit there in my pajamas, too close to the screen, squint at Peter Jennings. *I don't know where my sister is,* she says, *if she's okay at all. I love you very much,* she says, *don't leave your apartment if you don't have to.* I call my mother and she says, *You don't know what will happen tomorrow; don't be depressed about your life.* When I call my sister, she doesn't know yet, and I tell her, *terrorists, and hijacked planes, and thousands dead. Schools and city buildings in San Francisco are closed, and no foot traffic allowed on the Golden Gate Bridge. I have to go to the gynecologist,* she says. *I might have cervical tumors.* My friends call to check up on me. I watch the news. People say, *I'm freaked out, aren't you freaked out, we could go to war, this is the beginning of the end.* I say, *Yes, I'm freaked out. Yes, I can smell it, the promise of death. And I have seen it, the promise of a better life televised to the bad child.*

The Body as an Expression of Abuse

I want to talk now about my body and my relationship to it, that long vertical boat of a thing that never has enough water to rest in. I want to talk about the skin over my hands, and how I noticed again today the blue veins sticking out from underneath like vines pulsing beneath the thicket. Sometimes I lie in my bed wondering how I have inherited these aching muscles, these arms that want to cling to the mattress for hours until the sky darkens to a calm gray. Sometimes I walk next to a friend, and the only thing I can think of is how my body takes up space, space that does not seem to exist at all. My body is a quiet thing. I want to turn on a switch somewhere and light up a thousand eyes all over my skin. To feel every sensation, the sunlight flickering its thoughts upon me, strangers' words bouncing off my elbow, pelvis, a single lash uncurling. I carry my anxiety in my shoulders that always feel like heavy tires have screeched across the nerves there. I have bad posture. I often trip on the street. This is not a pity party; this is not a sad song. Yesterday, I ran for an hour around Stow Lake in Golden Gate Park. I had not run like that in years. I felt my feet complaining, and my lungs racing to catch up with my heart, which had left my body to race to the other end of the lake. My face felt hot. I knew it was bright red as if drunken from beer or *soju* [a Korean alcoholic beverage]. I heard my breath rushing past me, as if to race me.

I carry my fathers anger in my body. The impact of those blows, and the reverberations in these bones. I can't stand sudden noises, like the phone ringing, the buzz of the door-bell, people screaming, as they usually are, on Korean soap operas. I carry his disappointment in my ribs, the way they always feel too tightly wound, close to the center of my body, rather than facing out. I carry his words, the ones said in low tones, *This, is because I love you, this is because you need to know how to live in this world*—words so quiet sometimes there is no way of hearing them.

My father tells me, *Write poems that deal with how one may rejoice with sorrow.* I tell him, *There are other things to write about.* He tells me that's the trick in life, how to live with sadness in your heart, feeding off your blood. You can't go on if you give in to it, but you can't really live without it. I tell him that I will keep this in mind. Rejoice with sorrow. And I want to say, *I can never completely take your word for anything. No matter how learned you may be, no matter how well-lived and wise in the ways of life.* I remember his crazed eyes, the last time he tried to hit me. He lunged forward, an animal out of its cage and in search of prey. I kicked him in the stomach. I said things like, *You will not do this to me any-more,* And then all of a sudden, glass came shattering down somewhere, somewhere far away where the wreck would not harm us in the obvious physical way. We cut each other with words and looks and silences in between that cast the final votes. Daughter, father, what do these words mean for us now? Love, protection, promise—things kept in a closet hid-den behind the other things.

Nightmares

I grew up with nightmares. Men breaking into our house dressed in black leather carrying rifles or long knives. I always had to fight these intruders on my own since the rest of my family was usually asleep. It was like watching a movie, an image of me hiding behind the kitchen wall, waiting with a sharp knife in hand. The kitchen drawers were always cluttered, too many things inside them. I always wanted the biggest, sharpest knife. In these dreams, I usually won, successfully hacking off body parts and maiming the evildoers in their most critical organs. But every once in a while, I got knifed, or shot, though I never felt any of the pain. I grew up enacting these scenes over and over again, sometimes looking forward before sleep to the possibility of a new strategy. *Maybe this time I'll wait at the top of the stairs. Maybe I'll stand at the other side of the front door, and go crazy.* Now, I hardly remember dreams anymore. Usually they're not happy, but no longer as violent either. I have a lot of what Koreans would call "dog dreams" because they don't seem to make any sense at all. Last night, for instance, I waited for the elevator with a stranger. When the door opened, she turned to me and said, *Let's go in. This will take us straight to hell.* I rode the elevator up to her place, where she laid me down on her bed and kissed my dry, thirsty mouth. I think I wanted to say, *Stop, I don't want this*, but then the shock of her mouth on mine was so great I forgot words, thoughts, and when the phone rang in real life, I woke up, startled, felt the hard thing in my throat and pressed my hands to it, first letting my fingers brush quickly over my mouth.

SOCIAL ISSUES
FIRSTHAND

CHAPTER 2

Boys and Abuse

Verbal and Physical Abuse

Jim Van Buskirk

In this essay, Jim Van Buskirk remembers the many rituals of his childhood, from serving soup to shutting screen doors, which were supervised by his always critical mother. Yet while his father let himself be mothered, it was also he who administered the beatings. Reasons for this punishment were never given, and years later the author is still trying to overcome the effects of the random brutality. Jim Van Buskirk is the coauthor of Gay by the Bay: A History of Queer Culture in the San Francisco Bay Area.

"I'm serving the soup," my mother sang out cheerfully. Her voice bounced off the beige walls of the suburban house, enveloping and collecting my father, my brother, and me. Wherever we were, whatever we were doing, we heard her command: Come to the dinner table. Now.

My mother ladled Campbell's soup out of the Revere Ware pot into three turquoise Melmac [brand] bowls, and returned to the kitchen to set the pot back on the range. She stood tall and wide between the kitchen and the dining room until she had discerned that we all were indeed in our designated places at the table. Then she returned from the kitchen with the pot of reheated soup and ladled it into her own bowl. If there was a little extra, and only then, did she top off the soups already served.

"I like mine piping hot," she informed us, every evening. As if she needed to explain why we, the second-class citizens, had been summoned before she served herself.

I sat at the oblong Formica table, directly across from my mother. Along the other axis, the length of the table, sat my father and my brother. I faced my mother directly, head lowered, and glanced only occasionally in my father's direction. I usually ignored my annoying little brother.

The Dinner Rituals

As soon as the soup bowls were empty I sprang up to collect them and carry them into the kitchen. Now the bowls of iceberg lettuce moved center stage. A bottle of Wishbone Italian dressing was shaken, poured, and passed. Four times. Individually. After a few minutes of crunching, the contents of these bowls were dispensed with too.

Now came the main course. Tonight it was what my mother called Swiss steak. One of the few real recipes she made, it was chunks of potato and carrot and beef in a savory tomato sauce. She carefully spooned servings onto our plastic plates as we, her acolytes, held them toward her. She sat back and surveyed the table. We all bent our heads and began eating in earnest. It was delicious.

My Father Was Sick

Suddenly my father coughed.

Four forks froze. He coughed again. Our faces fell. My brother and I stopped breathing.

"Hold your arms over your head," my mother commanded, modeling the movement. My father's face reddened. Our faces went white; our eyes widened. Finally he breathed normally, and a sense of relief, release, ricocheted around the table. My mother felt obliged to explain what might have happened.

"You know, because your father had polio of the throat, he sometimes has trouble breathing. If he had continued to cough, I would have had to cut open his throat."

She told us this regularly, matter-of-factly, each time my father coughed. My mind immediately materialized the image of her getting up and going into the kitchen, pulling open the drawer where the carving knives were stored, and selecting a long, sharp knife.

My father nodded agreeably during this description of the narrowly averted disaster. If he so calmly acquiesced to her slitting his throat, what other choice did we have?

The first drama past, another command shot across the table. "Don't play with your food!" I looked up to see if it was directed at me, since I was older. I was relieved that this time my brother had intercepted her disdain.

"I'm mashing my potatoes," he explained.

"Well, don't make such a mess." She glared at him, then turned to me. "Tell Dad what you did in school today."

Daily Report

"Nothing," I mumbled. I had already told her all about my day as soon as I got home. Why would I want to repeat the story, even part of it, to my father? My father continued shoveling Swiss steak into his mouth, seemingly oblivious to the adjacent negotiations.

"Ed, show some interest," he was instructed. He looked up from his plate and pretended to pay attention, but still I refused to repeat any part of my recounting. But it wasn't a request. It was another way for my mother to exert control over the contents of the conversation. I decided to let her win this battle and offered up the *Reader's Digest* condensed version of my day. I waited while my mother interrupted me to add her perspective, or to betray confidences I'd shared earlier in the day, or to challenge me on my interpretation. It was as if it was all happening to someone else.

Not Enough Food

I reached for another spoonful of stew. "That's for my lunch," my mother stopped me.

"But I'm still hungry," I whined.

"If you're still hungry, you can have cold cereal."

I eyed the large covered casserole dish. Should I argue for more dinner, knowing I would lose, or acquiesce, and pour myself some cereal from the cupboard full of boxes and boxes of Cheerios, Wheaties, and Special K? Or, and this seemed the smartest solution, should I use this as an opportunity to be excused from the table?

"May I please be excused?" I obsequiously requested.

"I guess so," my mother agreed reluctantly.

I leaped from the table, eager to escape to the safety of my bedroom. So determined was I to depart that I had forgotten to inquire what was for "D." Whatever dessert might have been planned: canned fruit cocktail, instant butterscotch pudding, or Jell-O of some lurid color, it wasn't worth waiting for.

"Finish your homework," a final injunction flew down the hall.

"I will, I will," I assured her as I sprinted to my room, glad to have survived one more supper, one more serving of the soup.

Night Falls

"Close the screen door!"

I thought I was sneaking in slowly and quietly. But my mother, with eyes in the back of her head, as she so often reminded us, heard me enter through the back door. I carefully pulled shut the aluminum frame of the screen door.

"You'll let in mosquitoes," the disembodied maternal voice continued from afar. "And don't slam it."

I hated mosquitoes. Their buzzing noise loud around my ears as I tried to fall asleep drove me crazy. I didn't like it when I woke up in the morning with a bite or two, which I was repeatedly admonished not to scratch. But usually it was my younger brother who woke up bitten.

"It's because he's so sweet," my mother frequently explained.

What about me? Wasn't I sweet? I examined my arm and contemplated the buzzing bugs sucking blood from my brother's soft, white skin. Blood that would splat into the beige walls of the bedroom when we smashed a mosquito. The reddish brown smear on the wall was a symbol of a successful swat. Quickly, before mother saw it, we wiped it away with a Kleenex we moistened with spit. We knew to remove the evidence.

Who Am I?

Something else was also sucking our blood, but she didn't leave an itchy bump. This other vampire was slow, imperceptible. Unlike the mosquitoes, this one preferred my blood to my brother's.

As the screen door thudded shut, I padded across the cool linoleum floor, my bare feet suntanned on top, toughened below by a summer of hot asphalt streets and hotter beach sand, sometimes soothed by fresh green grasses, refreshing oceans, and suburban swimming pools.

I went into the hallway bathroom, shut the door, and locked it. After I peed, I let the faucet dribble a little water across my hands so that if questioned I could answer truthfully, yes, I had washed them.

I looked at myself in the mirror, but I couldn't hold the gaze. There was something about my face that reminded me of my mother. I tried to look into the eyes of this person, not a boy, not a man, who stared back at me. I couldn't figure out who he was. The inner me, the one no one knew about, or so I hoped, seemed to have nothing in common with the browned boy with blue eyes, the one whose face I wanted to know and like but from whom I felt oddly estranged.

It was a handsome face, according to my mother and my grandmother, but I didn't know what that meant. I didn't permit myself to know about handsome, for only boys were handsome and if I said a boy was handsome that would mean I'd looked at him, liked him, maybe even hoped he liked me. So to make sure I wasn't suspected of being like that, I never looked, not even at myself. Then neither I—nor my mother—

would know. That I was a boy not about baseball or racing cars, but about books and records, dreams and, yes, even love. Love: that elusive thing that I'd heard about, but never understood.

What Is Love?

"I've never been in love," my grandmother confided to me one afternoon. I was amazed. How could that be? I thought everyone had been in love, especially someone who had been married, even if she was now divorced and lived alone. My fourteen-year-old self was confused.

When I read about love, or saw it in movies, it seemed like a good thing: healing and happy and helping people become whole. In my own life it seemed horrible: malicious and manipulative and maddening. And most of the time it was all mixed up. So love was to be avoided as surely as looking at other boys, looking at myself.

Inspecting Myself

"What are you doing in there?" My mother's voice startled me out of my rumination.

"Uh, I'll be right out," I muttered, still facing the mirror.

My mother's mean glare came back at me from the mirror, out of my own eyes. "You are the most selfish person I know," she'd tell me repeatedly. And I tried to believe her, because my mother was always right, about everything. But I didn't feel selfish. I just felt like there were other things I wanted to do, places I wanted to escape to, someone else I wanted to be. But because she didn't want me to want those things, I was selfish.

Sometimes now when I look into a mirror, I see a strong, handsome face, one whose gaze I am able to hold. One I can imagine loving a little more, perhaps can even imagine letting be loved. Certainly not by my mother. But by another boy—I mean a man. A man like me, willing to risk coming out of the

31

locked bathroom, the stone tower, the hardened heart to see if it might be safe to share. A dream, or a hope, or a life.

Deception

Sometimes I recall my mother's recounting of what happened rather than the actual events.

Like the story of the ice cream. With great delight my mother repeatedly regaled us with how, when I was little, she and my father would go for ice cream. But because I made too much of a mess, she explained, I would be given an empty cone.

"You didn't realize the difference," she exclaimed happily.

But then, when my brother Rocky came along three and a half years later, the trick didn't work so well.

"He could tell right away that you had something he didn't." Almost lamenting that if it hadn't been for me and my ice cream, they could have continued the ruse with him. And also that he caught on much more quickly, than I had. I was apparently more than willing to accept their deceit—"No, dear, ours is just the same as yours."

I have known this story for years. Why now does it float to the surface of my consciousness? Because now I see it as a lie. One, that in my adoration of my parents, I was all too willing to believe, over my perception of the empty cone I was holding in my hand. And also because not only did it happen many times, I would have doubtless forgotten the episodes had they not been brought back to my attention, reinforcing the shame and humiliation that was my mother's well-honed modus operandi.

And I laughed at myself with her. I collaborated with her, laughed at the joke of my own naive trust, my stupidity, my belief that by being the protagonist in her story I was being attended to. That even though it made me feel queasy, being held up to ridicule was something I was willing to endure if it would buy me her love. I would keep quiet, would squelch the feelings that something was wrong, devastatingly wrong. I have kept quiet for nearly fifty years.

My Mother Lied Constantly

I learned to lie from my mother. Then I learned to lie to my mother. "I don't know where you get some of these ideas, dear," she cooed sweetly. I didn't either. I guess it was my way of trying to figure out how to fit together her lies with my truth.

I was good at jigsaw puzzles because I could see quickly both the shapes *and* the colors, could get a sense of the big picture *and* the tiny corner I was attempting to enlarge. It was like that with Mom too, except that every time I thought I'd made some progress toward figuring it out, the pieces would change shape, or the finished picture that had been the goal, actually finite and attainable, would change into a completely different picture and I'd have to start all over.

My mother didn't know she was telling lies. Repeatedly, destructively. Until recently, I gave her the benefit of the doubt, let her off the hook. After all, she'd been kidnapped by her father, taken at the age of six from her mother and her native land of France. She'd had to learn a new language, English, as a motherless child. I don't believe my mother ever understood the truth of what happened to her.

Lying to Myself

I remember my mother telling me proudly: "I was fifty before I could say the words: 'My father was an alcoholic.'" She'd already told us about carting away her father's empties as a teenager after dark so the neighbors wouldn't see. How did she expect us to believe that she hadn't known the truth?

I have spent my life lying to myself, believing my mother would have loved me if she'd been able to. Poor thing, she just didn't have it in her. Now I see it's more sinister than that. It is difficult for me to articulate other possible truths. I have to reinvent myself and my mother all at the same time.

I knew it wouldn't end up like Donna Reed, or Jane Wyatt on *Father Knows Best*, the weekly shows we watched religiously together as if we might get a glimpse of healing or wholeness or how to do it out of this small box that had only recently become a member of the family.

No Love

That wasn't the truth either, though I so desperately wanted it to be. So I lie to myself, telling myself the same lies my mother told me (and perhaps herself): Of course I love you. Of course I'm proud of you. It goes without saying.

Is that why I still don't know how to say it to myself? Don't know how to feel it might be the truth when I hear it from someone else? My mother is doubtless still telling herself lies. And I am trying to tell myself truths. Perhaps that is why we don't communicate, haven't spoken for years. May never, Harvey, my therapist, compassionately counsels me, be able to have a relationship.

With Harvey I have been working on sorting out the truths from the lies. Sometimes I still tell myself lies, and he lets me. But gradually my need to lie lessens, and slowly I see more clearly my truth.

Beatings

I was a good boy, probably too good. Then why was I whipped? What infractions of unspoken rules must I have inadvertently succumbed to?

When I tell people that I was frequently whipped, I always feel a current of electricity course through my body. I can't quite tell if it's warming or chilling, whether it makes me angry or sad, I just know it happens, every time. As if the pain and humiliation and unfairness are still embedded in my body after all these years. Shouldn't the energy have dissipated, run its course, gotten grounded?

Initially, I explain, it was with a belt, one taken from the many hanging in the closet. Or, if time was of the essence, from around my father's waist, coiling like a snake preparing to strike. Later he used a dog whip he'd inherited (perhaps from his father), which hummed as he ripped it through the air with relish.

"Go lie down and get ready for your spanking."

Even as I write these words the shame washes up my neck and out the top of my head. So I'd dutifully lie down on my own corduroy-covered bed, the one whose bolsters turned it into what my mother called a "Hollywood sofa." I liked the sound of that name; it went well with my fixation on Hollywood movies and their stars.

Punishment

So I lay face down, my pants and underpants pulled past my knees, in preparation, as I had been taught. And waited. Waited, wondering what I had done to deserve discipline in such a fashion. It must have been something serious because my parents wouldn't insist on inflicting it if it wasn't absolutely necessary. Would they? I wondered as I lay there. My parents loved me, of that I was sure. Wasn't their whipping me "for my own good," as they always reminded me, proof of that? Weren't they trying to teach me right from wrong, like they told me, to make sure I would always be a good boy?

Finally my father entered the room. He asked if I understood why I was being beaten. I lied and said yes. And as he took the strap to my white uncovered legs, I kept myself from crying, from giving him the satisfaction of knowing that he'd betrayed me, believing my mother's version of what happened before mine. Believing, as she wanted him to, that I was bad. Not that I had exhibited bad behavior, but was intrinsically bad, so bad that the evil needed to be beaten out of me. So if they both believed it, what other choice did I have but to believe it too? I buried that belief deep in my body, by not crying, by not allowing myself to hate them.

Physical Memories

One recent afternoon at Esalen [Esalen Institute is renowned for natural hot springs]. I treated myself to a massage. I couldn't really afford it, having spent so much on my weekly visits to the psychotherapist, the massage therapist, the acupuncturist. But I was there in hopes of healing something I wasn't able to identify. Some tactile tissue contact, something I seldom get, seemed necessary.

Peter, the masseur, came to collect me from the hot tub where I had been soaking. I told him about my pain as we walked to the massage yurt. He listened carefully to the descriptions of the throbbing, aching, tingling, and numbness that continually ran from my neck and shoulders down my left arm and into my hand. He listened sympathetically as I quickly chronicled the visits to the chiropractor, osteopath, and neurosurgeon, and the unsuccessful attempts to ameliorate the pain with drugs. He gently helped me lie down on the massage table. Sometimes even this simple position is painful, but today the discomfort was minimal. As Peter reached under my body and pressed up into spots across my back, the discomfort turned to pain, and then intensified. It quickly became excruciating.

Humiliation

I felt my eyes squeeze tight with the pain. Surely he noticed my agony, but he pressed on, igniting spasms of burning that built on each other until I couldn't stand it anymore. I was lifted out of my body on a canopy of pain. From that raised perspective I looked down and saw not a forty-eight-year-old man being massaged but my father whipping his eight-year-old son. I felt the sting of the whip, the humiliation of knowing it was intended for dogs. And then, rising higher in the paroxysms of pain, I saw my father's father beating him, perhaps with the same whip. Of course, how could it be otherwise? And though I couldn't actually see it, I imagined my grandfather being beaten by his father.

From there I plunged back into my body, even below it. It was like I was on a carnival ride of pain. I felt my arm freeze and my hand go numb. Had I made a terrible mistake? Had my massage transformed the pain into permanent paralysis?

Usually I don't want my massages to end; I thought this one never would. Finally it did. And slowly as I began to breathe, sensation came back into my body. Oily now, I was surprised to find that I didn't feel any worse for my workout. Was it my imagination that I actually had a bit more mobility, a bit less pain? Or was it only that I'd found part of the answer to my unanswerable question of why I was whipped?

Shallow Breathing

"Exhale!" Roy, my burly body worker, exhorted. "Good. Now do it with your mouth open. That's going to be your homework."

"That's always my homework," I counter in a combination of adult sarcasm and childish complaint. I never even realized that I don't breathe. Well, of course I breathe, but it's very shallow, and my mouth usually remains closed. It's as if I don't want to get caught breathing, don't want to get caught, period. Don't trust that there will be enough air for my next breath.

Roy asks me if it's all right if Jack, a student intern, sits in on our weekly session. Oh sure, I say blithely. I have conveniently forgotten that the only other time Jack "sat in" was a few weeks ago: he held my shoulders down on the table while I raised my knees to my chest and Roy pushed my bent legs over toward the table until my vertebrae exploded "popopopop" like a string of Chinese firecrackers. Immediately, I burst into spontaneous laughter.

"Fire," Roy explained to Jack. Then they twisted me to the left side. More uncontrollable laughter.

It doesn't dawn on me that today the process is to be repeated. When I realize what's about to happen, I inadvertently hold my breath. After instructing Jack, Roy tells me, "Your job is to breathe." Together they perform the adjustment on my spine.

"Popopopop." Fewer firecrackers this time, and no laughter. Just an ongoing series of deep exhalations, one right after another. After allowing me a few moments to recover, they twist me to the left. This side isn't as explosive, but the deep exhalations continue.

Grieving

Roy mentions grieving, a topic we have often discussed. He suggests that there might be some tears mixed into the exhalation, but I find none. I realize I don't know how to grieve. I can cry, but it's not the same thing. Earlier that week, faced with the return of a story I thought had been accepted into an anthology, I didn't know what to do: Get drunk? Call a friend and complain? Play songs I knew would elicit tears? Go to bed? It was ten o'clock and I was tired, so I chose the last of my narrow range of options, and collapsed into a deep sleep.

But the next day I realized it wasn't only the disappointment of the rejected story. I was also starting to acknowledge rejection by a man I had been spending time with. He seemed to see me, and I thought our intellectual connection was slowly leading to one of emotional and/or physical intimacy. Though the messages had been mixed I was finally forced to face the fact that he wasn't interested, at least not as interested as I was, not as interested as I wanted him to be. And so without shedding a tear, while Roy and Jack watched, I exhaled and exhaled and exhaled.

As I put on my shirt, I mentioned to Roy that my resistance to exhaling was related to my fear of inhaling, having to replenish my air supply with a fresh batch.

Never Enough Air

As I drove home, I remembered taking scuba diving lessons years ago. It took a long time to assemble and climb into the equipment: wet suit, mask, snorkel, fins, air tank. . . . Even though I was thin, I wore more than the estimated number of lead weights on the weight belt. Nevertheless I continually bobbed to the surface. More weights were woven into the belt around my narrow waist and still I wouldn't sink. I finally realized that it was because I was afraid of completely exhaling, of voiding my body of used air in order to refill it with a fresh supply from the tank on my back. I had checked the gauges, the O-ring, the regulator mouthpiece, and still I was afraid. Afraid that after exhaling there would be no air to inhale. So I kept my breaths shallow, breathing a little out and a little in. Eventually, involuntarily, I floated to the surface of the water, away from the other divers.

With Roy's repetitious reminders, I am getting better at breathing, getting ready to begin grieving. It's as if I need to be continually convinced that there is an inexhaustible supply of air around me. Fresh, sweet, restorative, purging, healing air. It's the concept of porosity, Harvey has noted. My systems, emotional and physical, are so controlled that nothing gets in and nothing gets out. The air just stays in my body along with the grief. I'm trying to trust that there will be enough air to breathe in, trust that it will be safe to exhale the grief.

When my trust in my air supply is more secure, maybe I will decide to dive deep into disappointment. I'm still afraid I'll be overwhelmed, still don't know whether I'll sink or swim in this sea of sorrow. For now I stay in the shallow end and give myself permission not to grieve. Then I take a deep breath, and exhale.

Father-Son Incest

Jimmy, as told to Michel Dorais

In this selection, Jimmy tells how he was being ignored by his dad, until one day his father started to sexually abuse him. Only after forcing him into sex, did the older man take an interest in his son. After becoming physically stronger than his dad, the abuse stopped, and when Jimmy entered a group home, he finally confronted his father, Yet his problems have not stopped there, and his family continues to downplay the abuse. Today Jimmy is still trying to come to terms with who he is and where he belongs. Jimmy's full name is withheld to protect his identity.

I was always rejected by my father because I wasn't how he wanted me to be. I had problems at school because of that. I was supersensitive and cried all the time if the other kids picked on me, or if things just didn't go right. The other boys laughed at me because of this. They called me names. My father wasn't proud of me; he didn't talk to me. The only place I could be alone at home was in my own room. My dad didn't allow me to watch TV: he said I hadn't earned it. He was really strict and his rules were rigid. I was reprimanded for being the slightest bit late. To punish me, he took away my toys. I played with my socks instead. I pretended they were animals, trucks, people. My mother acted as a go-between. She tried to prevent my being punished or hit but she avoided contradicting him, so he wouldn't turn on her perhaps.

As a child I was unhappy. I looked at the fathers of my friends and wondered if mine was normal. He never played with me, never did sports with me. People think an only child is spoiled. Well, it wasn't true for me. My grandparents spoiled me from time to time. My parents didn't have much money, and they didn't give me very much. Maybe they regretted having me. Then again, my father really had it in for his parents because they hadn't paid for his education, so maybe it pissed him off to see them spoiling me.

I had trouble getting along with other kids. I was jealous of them, with their great toys and the attention they got from their parents. I missed out on all that. I tried to understand my father's money problems, but it didn't change anything.

He Abused Me

The first time it happened, I had just turned seven. One evening, my father came into my room with a flashlight. He came close, sat down on my bed, and started touching me. I mean abusing me. I didn't understand and I didn't try to understand what was going on. Right then, I thought it was part of a game, that all children did this. He fondled me, he lay down and rubbed himself against me. He said not to tell my mother about it. He said he wasn't doing it to be wicked. I didn't trust my father after he asked me to lie.

I didn't know too much about sex. I was never taught anything about it. I didn't know how to react. I obeyed my father. My mother never suspected anything. It wasn't really regular, just once in a while. He'd ask me to go to his room when my mother wasn't there, right up until I was about thirteen. It was about once a month. I didn't count how often.

I didn't like him touching me but those were the only times he took any notice of me unless he was punishing me. After he came, he'd light a cigarette, talk to me, ask me questions—he'd ask why it wasn't going well at school, or at home. We'd rough-house on the bed like two friends: for once he was nice. It was as though I had to allow myself to be abused to be worth talking to. As soon as he got out of bed, he was the same as before. He treated me like an object, a thing. I was his thing.

Resistance

Towards the end, when I began to refuse, he said to me: "Don't expect me to be nice with you in future." I started asking myself questions when I had my first girlfriend. I was finding it difficult to have a girlfriend while continuing to have sex with my father. I had understood what my father was doing. From that time on, I tried to resist him. He would begin to fondle me but I would say no. Faced with my lack of cooperation, he finally left me alone.

When I was little, each time I did the smallest thing wrong, I knew my father would beat me or punish me. I used to cry at the sight of him, right up until I was a teenager. Later I became aggressive towards him. My mother told me to settle things with him myself, that I was big enough. So the next time he tried to hit me, I stood up to him and defied him: "Go on! Hit me!" He walked off and didn't touch me. Before, I used to throw myself on the floor when he hit me. Now I was standing up to him, as if I wasn't afraid of him any more. He was a man who could be violent and kick me in the ribs, throw things at me, hit me with his fists. As soon as I felt stronger, more confident, I began to be less respectful towards him, to yell and scream my head off as he used to do. I saw my father as the enemy, as my worst enemy. He said: "Obey me. I'm your father." I replied: "A father doesn't behave the way you do."

Difficulties with Girls

The first time I kissed my first girlfriend I was embarrassed. I was wondering about my father. Why does he do that? Between my girlfriend and my father—how is it different? What does my father mean to me? At that age you begin to hear about homosexuals. I said to myself I was not homosexual, that I went out with girls. But my father. . . . Why does he do that? On the other hand, he's not gay. . . . I realized that my friends didn't have this kind of relationship with their fathers, that they didn't have the problems I had.

During all those years I never spoke about what was happening. No one knew about it. When there was talk about love or about sex at school, I was embarrassed. I really had no experience of that. I knew very little about girls. I had my first sexual encounters with girls at fourteen or fifteen. When I was making love, I tried not to think of my father, but interfering images constantly came to me. I found myself to be awkward sexually and it upset me not to know how to go about it. The fact that I had finally been able to refuse my father reassured me. Today, in my encounters with girls I'm the one who makes the decisions. They have to go along with me, not force me. I prefer girls who are more passive because they must take me as I am. I'm not easy, I'm often argumentative. If I go without having a girl for a while, it worries me. I ask myself if I'll be able to find another.

Living in a Foster Home

As for guys, I don't trust them. I was friends with this twenty-four-year-old guy who worked in the foster home I was placed in after the incest was disclosed. I got very attached to him. He was like a substitute father. He invited me to his place to look at films, do whatever I liked. He taught me music, took me out. I was fourteen. He had become my best friend. Then I discovered he was gay. I had noticed that he only invited guys to his place. Even though he hadn't done anything bad with me, this discovery set off an alarm inside me. I stopped talking to him and made fun of him with my friends. I broke off all contact with him. Today, if a homosexual approaches me he's likely to lose a few teeth. . . .

I myself have trouble understanding who I am. I've become intolerant and weepy; I have an unstable personality. I find I'm quite isolated. Taking drugs hasn't helped. I tell myself I've become like my father. That really disheartens me.

After I was sent to the group home, I decided to disclose my incest in order not to become a perpetrator myself. I found myself there because I was stealing from shops. I was doing it for the risk, for the challenge, for the mixture of fear and pleasure. Once at the group home, I spilled the beans. I decided to take my father to court for what he had done. I was hesitant, but my social worker encouraged me and arranged for me to meet with a lawyer. I told myself it was good for me and it would help my father too. I made a declaration where I recounted everything. They arrested my father. He owned up. Today he is on probation.

No Family Support

I haven't seen my father again. I didn't have to testify because he pleaded guilty. I've had no news of him since then, only from my mother. My relationship with her became very cold for several months. My father worked her up against me, but then she was mad at me for my drug habit too. As for her, she wants to help my father. She minimizes the seriousness of what he's done. The other day, on the telephone, she said to me: "Anyway, it's not like he abused ten people; you were the only one." That hurt me, hearing that. As if what I had gone through didn't count. When I told her what had been going on, she told me she had suspected something without knowing exactly what. She didn't know whether to believe me. The more time passed, the less she believed me, because of my behaviour problems. I don't find it right, what she's doing. She tells me stupid things, tries to blame me, to make me believe that it's my fault, what happened. The last time we talked, I overdosed on mescaline the next day.

My father is afraid of going to jail. He has bad memories of the one night he spent there. His relationship with my mother has changed. He no longer has that strong man image. Now it's my mother who wears the trousers. As for me, I'm quite lost in all of this and just want to cry when I think about it. I wonder whether I could love my father in spite of everything. I have to force myself to say I don't love him. And I feel guilty myself. Do I love him? Do I not love him? It's hard to figure out.

Identity Crisis

The longer this goes on the more depressed I get. Who am I? I don't know. I dont know why it happened, either. If my father hadn't abused me I wouldn't be here, in a group home. I would be sitting at home, I'd be okay. Basically, all the problems I've had are due to him, to what he did to me. I don't accept it. I lost my childhood because of him. Now I'm losing my adolescence. Will I lose my whole life like that? I might just as well finish it right now.

But there is something positive in my life right now. I'm learning music, and I'm writing poetry and songs. I have projects with my friends. I'd like to study music or literature. I'm getting ahead little by little. It's encouraging to see that people find me talented. I ask myself whether they mean it.

Children? No, I don't want any. I don't want to get married either: it's not worth it. My parents haven't exactly been a good example. I would like to have a girlfriend, but children, no. I don't want a complicated life. I would like to be wealthy, to be free of problems, live on my own mountain, be able to watch the people down below without them being able to hurt me. The worst thing for a guy who's been abused is confusion, mixed with fear of what's going to happen; that's on top of the despondency and low morale. Even your reasoning is no longer what it should be. Sometimes I don't understand what people are trying to say to me. I don't understand what they are doing. . . .

I Can't Be Myself

I put on a tough front. People think I'm hard but I'm just acting a role, like in a drama. I identify to a great extent with Jim Morrison of The Doors. I would love to make music and write like him. The essential is that I will have to be myself. But it's as though I no longer have an identity, that I'll have to glue one on, so to speak. I do have a made-up identity, but it's only a role I play. It's hard for boys like me to find out who they really are. I identify with Jim Morrison because I sense he went through the same thing I did. His behaviour, his problems with his father, and his mother too, it makes me think of someone who has suffered incest. He was turned inward on himself, and he wrote, like I do. We have a lot in common. He bore an image: The Lizard King [Morrison's persona—a name taken from one of his poems. As for me, I bear the image of an image.

Abused by a Priest

John Salveson

In this text John Salveson describes the years of abuse he suffered at the hands of a widely loved and admired priest, Father Robert Huneke. For years he molested Salveson, and when the teenager finally left for college, Father Huneke transferred to the University of Notre Dame to continue the abuse. When Salveson finally went public, the Catholic authorities reacted first with silence, then with scorn, never acknowledging nor apologizing for the priest's actions. John Salveson is one of twelve plaintiffs in a lawsuit filed against the diocese of Rockville Centre, New York.

Almost 30 of us were at that March meeting in New Jersey. We were sharing our experiences as survivors of clergy abuse and discussing ways we could work together to help the victims of that abuse.

The Attorney General of New Jersey and the Executive Director of the U.S. Conference of Catholic Bishops' Office of Child and Youth Protection were there to listen. The five bishops who lead the five dioceses that make up New Jersey also were invited. None of them showed up. The absence of the bishops led me to reflect on how little has changed with the Roman Catholic Church since the clergy abuse scandal erupted in 2002.

In June 2002, the U.S. Conference of Catholic Bishops approved its landmark Charter for the Protection of Children and Young People. Among other things, the charter requires that each diocese reach out to victims of clergy abuse, that offending priests be removed from ministry and that the church conduct itself with "transparency" when it deals with this scandal.

John Salveson, "I Was Abused," *Notre Dame Magazine Online*, summer 2003. Reproduced by permission.

Despite these promises, . . . [t]he Diocese of Detroit took nine months to investigate a priest accused of abusing two women; a priest convicted of trafficking in child pornography continued to serve in a Philadelphia parish; a Delaware priest who admitted to sexual abuse of a student was hired by the Archdiocese of Chicago to rewrite liturgies and was housed in the cardinals mansion next door to an elementary school. And on it goes.

Reasons for Involvement

Friends and family members frequently ask me why I continue my very public and personal efforts to support victims of clergy abuse and to expose the behavior of the church whose priests abused them. I often ask myself this question as well.

I always come back to three reasons. First, in my view the Catholic church continues to deliberately and profoundly fail in doing the right thing to support the victims of its priests' sexual abuse. Second, when I speak of my own abuse, other abuse victims come out of their isolation and darkness and try to get help. Finally, it helps me to cope with and integrate the effects of the sexual abuse I suffered for seven years at the hands of a Catholic priest.

This is my story. There is nothing about it, or me, that is extraordinary or unusual. Multiply it by a couple of thousand, and you will begin to understand the devastating impact clergy sexual abuse has on its victims and the church.

The Abuse

I grew up on Long Island in New York, part of a standard-issue, middle-class, Catholic family. I attended Catholic school starting in the third grade (my mother couldn't get the pastor to let me in earlier, as there were already more than 50 kids in the class). I was a kid any parent would be happy to have. I worked hard in school, stayed out of trouble and was involved in my church. I went through a long period as a child when I aspired to be a priest. I can still remember being fascinated by the book *The Making of a Priest*, which I would read at night under the covers of my bed with the aid of a flashlight, when I was supposed to be asleep.

The summer before I began attending my parish high school, Saint Dominic, in 1969, I met Father Robert Huneke, a new priest in our parish. He was young, smart, funny and sarcastic. He had us call him Father Bob and quickly became popular among my church and school friends.

Father Bob spent most of his time with young people. He was the sponsor of our Folk Mass group and was instrumental in getting us all to sign up for "Christian Awakening," a weekend retreat program involving several Long Island parishes. He let us smoke cigarettes around him and criticized the other parish priests in front of us. He swore. He was like no other priest I had ever met.

My parents were thrilled to have Father Bob in the picture. He quickly became close to my family. I saw him in school, on weekends at Mass and on weekday evenings at Christian Awakening or Folk Mass practice. Sometimes he would come to our home for dinner.

In fall 1969, Father Bob invited me to go with him on a weekend trip to Virginia to visit a family that had moved out of our parish. I jumped at the chance. I was 13 years old and incredibly impressed with myself for being invited on such a trip.

Father Bob and I shared a bedroom at the home in Virginia. During the night, he got into my bed and began to perform oral sex on me. As I awoke, I became terrified and stunned. I was profoundly shocked, without any idea of how to react to his behavior.

The next morning, we left the home in Virginia and started the drive back to New York. Over breakfast, Father Bob told me that what "we" did was okay. He explained that it was okay to show love for each other, and that God accepted and encouraged it. I was nearly unable to speak. I remember feeling responsible for the abuse almost immediately. I also remember feeling nauseated. I had absolutely no idea what to do. It never occurred to me to tell another adult what happened.

Years of Dependency

As time went on, the abuse continued. Father Bob was expert at making me feel special and completely dependent on him. I was also terrified of him and lived for his approval. He was a priest. I felt that I had no choice but to do exactly what he wanted. He used his considerable influence over me to be sure I continued to comply.

This was the start of seven years of sexual abuse, which included most any sexual activity between two males that you can imagine. Through all of this, I took frequent trips with Father Huneke and often spent time in his room in the rectory. We drank a great deal of alcohol. This helped me cope, and I was kind of proud that I could tell the difference between Johnnie Walker Black Label Scotch and Johnnie Walker Red Label by age 15.

While he had considerable control over my body, Father Huneke had complete control over my mind. He told me it was all right to do this with him and that God approved. If I balked, he told me it meant that I was unloving, ungrateful and cold. He often told me I was a "bad person" if I did not do exactly what he wanted. I believed him. He was a priest. I had somehow allowed him to hijack my entire view of myself. If he thought I was okay, I was okay. If he thought I was bad, I was crushed and depressed.

Developing Two Personalities

He also drummed into me his personal view of what it meant to be a "good person." He often repeated his view of the world to me: "Life is a sh— sandwich, and every day you take another bite." He said being a good Christian meant having a difficult life. Consequently, the more miserable a person was in his life, the better a Christian he was. His abuse was making me extremely miserable, so I believed I was living the right kind of Christian life.

During this time I began to develop into two people—the abused John, terrified and unable to get help, and the public John. I was a leader in my high school, an editor of the school paper, leader of the parish Folk Mass group, an ice hockey player and ultimately president of my senior class. I was not some strange kid in the shadows. Any mother in that parish would have been thrilled to have me date her daughter.

I moved easily between these two people. When I was not with Father Bob, I tried not to think of him or of what was going on. But it hung over me like a cloud. I was always anxious about what Father Bob was thinking of me, and if I was going to have to go to his room for a long "talk," which he frequently required.

Going Away to College

I entered Notre Dame [in Indiana] as a freshman in fall 1973. Part of my agenda in moving so far from New York was to get away from Father Huneke. He visited a few times, despite my efforts to keep him away. When he came to the campus, he would stay at the Morris Inn, where the abuse continued. I occasionally was able to avoid him. He would suggest trips during breaks from school, and I created conflicting plans. This would anger him, but I managed to limit my time with him. That became harder when he announced, in 1974, that he was coming to Notre Dame to be an assistant rector at Cavanaugh Hall and enter graduate school for a master's degree in psychological counseling, which he received in 1976.

When he arrived, I tried to stop the sexual activity in the relationship. I would resist him and tell him I couldn't continue. He responded in one of two ways. One was the screaming, angry Father Bob, who told me how ungrateful I was for all he had done for me. The other was the tearful, pitiful Father Bob, who told me no one else loved him in the world but me. Both worked.

I was devastated, depressed and petrified that he was coming to Notre Dame, but what could I do? He ended up staying for the remainder of my Notre Dame years, eventually becoming rector of Grace Hall. His control over my self-esteem and decision-making continued to be as complete as ever. He insisted that I serve as a resident assistant in his dormitory. As a senior, I left Alumni Hall and became an R.A. [resident assistant] at Grace. After six years of this abusive relationship, I was simply unable to create enough sense of self to say no to this assignment. Still, I hated the idea of doing it.

At the start of my senior year, I told Father Huneke I could no longer allow our relationship to continue. I had tried this many times before, but his shouting or crying always won me over. This time I was done. I was 20 years old, and I'd had it. He threatened to fire me, treated me horribly and tried all of his old tricks. I was so disgusted with myself that I didn't care anymore. I wanted it to be over. He never touched me again.

Moving On

I stayed at Notre Dame to get a graduate degree and then moved to Philadelphia in 1978. I arrived with no friends, a professional job and a good-sized drinking problem. I was engaged at the time to a woman who was a year behind me at Notre Dame, but it was not going well. We eventually ended the relationship. I was on my own.

It wasn't until I entered a serious relationship with the woman who would become my wife that I began to realize the nature of my relationship with Father Bob. I had done my best to forget about it, but I found that it continued to haunt me. As I spoke to my future wife, Susan, about what happened, it began to dawn on me that I was not the responsible party. I had been abused and taken advantage of. It came to me slowly. It helped explain my horrible bouts with depression and my relationship problems. It also helped explain my unlimited anger against the Catholic church and all it stood for. I still wasn't ready, however, to make the connection between my prodigious drinking and the abuse.

In 1980, at age 24, I understood that the relationship with Father Huneke was more than just a strange aspect of my life. It was abuse, and it was having a major effect on my life as an adult. As I tried to deal with its impact through therapy, I began to think about what Father Huneke was currently doing. Was he still abusing other people? Was he still at Notre Dame? I became obsessed with stopping him and protecting any future victims.

Contacting the Authorities

I wrote to Bishop John McGann of the Diocese of Rockville Centre on Long Island in 1980, telling him of my abuse and asking him to let me know what had happened to Father Huneke. I shared my concern about other potential victims and told him of the devastating effect the abuse had on my life. I did not ask the bishop for money or support of any kind. I just wanted him to be aware that he had an abusive priest in his diocese, and that I wanted the priest to be removed, treated or monitored in some way.

Bishop McGann did not reply to my letter. So I sent another, this time registered mail. I got a call from his secretary, who set up a meeting between the bishop and myself. We met on Long Island in summer 1980. The bishop seemed sympathetic and supportive. I did notice that he was uncomfortable with our talk, but who wouldn't be? God knows I was. He promised to "take care of it."

That meeting began a nine-year battle to have Huneke removed from active ministry. During those nine years, the bishop moved the priest from parish to parish. He assigned him to an all-boys high school. We corresponded: I insisted that the church needed to remove Huneke, and the bishop insisted that there were no other victims and I should let it be. I knew there were other victims—in fact, the bishop wrote me that Father Huneke told him that "this matter" had not been a problem for two years (since 1978). His abuse of me ended in 1976. By his own admission, there were other victims. The bishop didn't want to hear about it.

Going Public

In 1988, I decided that the only way I would get the diocese to take action against Father Huneke was to expose his abuse publicly. Before I did so, I knew I had to tell my parents and brothers of my abuse. Up to that time, only a few people in my life knew what had happened to me. With my therapist's and my wife's encouragement, I told my parents. Both were, and are, active, committed Catholics. They were devastated, angry and confused. But they supported me, as did my brothers.

My first attempt to "go public" and expose the abuse involved speaking to a reporter at *Newsday*, Long Island's most widely read newspaper. The paper wouldn't publish the story. The reporter, a religion writer assigned to the story, told me I seemed more like some sort of "teacher's pet" to her than an abuse victim. The editors suggested that if I located other victims they might consider an article. That evening I took out my high school yearbook and began to call people I suspected might also have been abused. By the end of the evening, I had a list of about 10 other victims of Father Huneke.

The newspaper was still uncomfortable with the story, despite my new revelations. I gave up on *Newsday* and explored whether I could sue the church as a way to expose them. I spoke to a few lawyers, and they told me I had no chance to litigate. One told me that if I were a "drooling idiot" whose life had been irreparably harmed by the abuse I might have a chance. He was concerned that I was too normal—married with three children and a successful career. Where was the harm?

The Pepetrator Is Exposed

Finally, I decided that the only way to remove the priest was to do it myself. I wrote an open letter to the parishioners of the parish in which Father Huneke served, telling them of my abuse and their bishop's knowledge of it for nine years. My father and two brothers and I stood outside his church on a Sunday morning in July 1989 and handed the letter to people as they left Mass. I had called the television news outlets, and NBC had a camera crew and reporter at the church. They captured the near-riot that ensued as parishioners shouted at us to leave the church grounds. Parishioners attacked the cameraman, injuring him, and tried to grab the microphone from the reporter. The dramatic story was the lead for both the 6 and 11 o'clock news that evening in New York. The diocese issued a meaningless statement. But the priest was removed. He had actually been reassigned a few weeks earlier, when *Newsday* had called the diocese regarding the story they were considering. But he was finally gone. It had taken me nine years.

I met a few weeks later with an angry Monsignor John Alesandro, chancellor of the Diocese of Rockville Centre. He berated me for the actions I had taken but said the priest finally had been confronted. Father Huneke had admitted to his abuse of me and supplied a list of other victims.

I Was the Enemy

During this nine-year period of trying to expose the priest, I faced many difficult questions. What would it do to my relationship with my parents and brothers to tell them of the abuse? What about all my aunts, uncles and cousins—all committed Catholics? How would they react? What about my work? My career was beginning to take off. Did I really want to become known as a victim of sexual abuse by a priest? What would my clients say?

What if the church sued me? What if Huneke sued me? The reason my wife didn't hand out the letters with me that morning was because I was advised by a lawyer that if she wasn't there with me, and we got sued by the church and lost, at least we could probably keep our home—since it was joint property. These were the kinds of decisions I faced in deciding to go public.

Through it all, the church in which I grew up, the Roman Catholic Church, treated me like the enemy. No one ever apologized for what their priest did to me. In fact, no one ever even admitted in writing that he had abused me. No one ever asked how my life was or what effect it had on my family and me. No one offered to pay for my therapy or speak to my despondent, grieving parents. No one asked me about my spiritual life and whether this had shaken my faith in God. Diocesan officials reached out to only one other victim abused by Huneke. They told him he could get free counseling with a priest at Catholic Social Services. He declined. The rest they ignored. To this day, in 2003, they have never done any of these things.

My Life Today

I subscribe to the "baggage" theory of mental health. I believe we all enter adulthood with a certain amount of emotional baggage from our families and early life experiences. Some of us have very little, others a fair amount. My experience is that abuse victims enter adulthood with steamer trunks on their backs.

What kind of baggage did I get? Poor self-esteem. Depression. A belief that I will be "found out" as an imposter and that I have fooled everyone into thinking I am a capable, healthy person. Relationship challenges. Trouble with intimacy. Difficulty with authority figures. A sense of humor that can be a little too biting. Alcoholism.

Part of my baggage theory is that you can shed baggage as you progress through life or you can choose to keep it and slog along. I've tried to shed as much of mine as I can. I've worked through a lot of these things, with a lot of help from a lot of people, and will continue to do so. Actually, I consider myself incredibly lucky and certainly not worthy of or interested in pity. I have a wonderfully supportive wife and three terrific children, whom I love and who love me. My parents and brothers have supported me without question. I am a partner in a successful business. I've been given the gift of sobriety. Life is good.

Dedicated to Change

But I can't sit on the sidelines and watch the Catholic church resist doing the right thing. A large part of me wants to let it go, to forget about it. Many people have advised me to do so. But I feel a strong personal, ethical responsibility to help other survivors and to try to hold the church accountable. It borders on obsession at times and takes its toll in my personal life.

Today, I volunteer as the regional director of the Philadelphia Chapter of SNAP (Survivors Network of those Abused by Priests). SNAP is dedicated to helping heal survivors of clergy abuse and works to hold the church accountable for its actions.

I became active in SNAP in 2002 as the crisis got the attention I expected it to get in 1989. I went to Dallas to be with other survivors at the U.S. bishops' conference. I began to talk to the media again. I was featured in an article in *Newsday* and also in the local Philadelphia media. I truly became and continue to be public about my abuse.

I now meet new victims regularly. I also meet the parents and spouses of victims whose loved ones have not been able to deal with their abuse and are ruining their lives and families. Many are just coming out, after years of hiding and denial. Their stories are outrageous and heartbreaking and fuel my anger.

Virtually every person I have ever met whom a Catholic priest has abused has gone to the church for help. I have never met one who felt the church took care of him or her properly. Instead, the victims have been lied to, ignored, berated, condemned and mistreated. We even have a word for it—revictimization. It is a common experience. A small handful have sued the church and won. Most have given up, bested by the lowest form of hardball legal tactics employed by the church. The Catholic church continues to behave with arrogance and aloofness. . . .

What has driven us from the church are our experiences with the bishops and cardinals who supported and sheltered the abusive priests. There is nothing so devastating for a victim as going to the church for help and being treated as a legal adversary. I am not referring to victims who sue the church. They are at least partially ready for the treatment they receive. I am talking about the vast majority of victims who go to the church for help. What they want is simple and inexpensive. First, they want the church to acknowledge that they were abused by one of their clergy. Second, they want an apology. Third, they often want some help paying for the resources they need to try to get their lives back.

The thing they want the most, however, is the thing that is most scarce. They want the church to reach out to them with compassion and support. They want to be folded into the arms of the church and nurtured and supported through recovery. They want to be asked how they are doing, how their family is coping, how their parents are. They want someone to put aside the concern for the image of the church and focus instead on helping them to heal. In my 23 years of working on this issue, I have never met a person who has had this experience with the church, or anything even approximating it.

A Simple Solution

The solution to this crisis is simple and inexpensive. However, it requires a fortune in courage and moral commitment.

The bishops and cardinals who shielded, supported and protected the abusive priests in their midst need to acknowledge their actions and have the integrity and courage to step aside. The people who step into their shoes need to reach out to the survivors of abuse, welcome them into the church and find out what they can do to help them. They need to proactively inquire into the spiritual and emotional health of the survivors and their families. They need to do whatever it takes to get them well—through therapy and support in their parishes. They need to let every member of their diocese know the names of the priests who have abused children and try to find out if there are other victims of those priests who have not yet come forward. They need to invite victims of abuse to come to their churches to speak to the parishioners about their experiences. They need to stop parsing words, splitting hairs and listening to their lawyers. They need to settle their lawsuits with victims fairly and quickly.

If the church had done these things when the victims of its abuse had first come forward, it would have avoided the millions of dollars worth of lawsuits it has incurred. Its bishops and cardinals would also be sleeping better at night, and its good and holy priests, who are legion, would not be so embarrassed to be priests in the Roman Catholic Church. It would still have the voice of moral authority and credibility in America, rather than being a punch line for late-night comics. And people like me, who went to them for help, could say to ourselves "I was abused, which was awful, but I was saved and nurtured by my church when I came forward."

An Apology

In 1996, I was traveling by train from Washington, D.C., to Philadelphia. When I got on the train in Union Station, I saw Father Hesburgh [the longtime president of Notre Dame] sitting by a window with an empty seat next to him. I quickly took the seat and introduced myself as an alum. As the train pulled out of the station, Father Hesburgh began to regale me with stories from his life at Notre Dame. As he spoke, all I could think of was whether I should tell him what happened to me, to see what he thought about it. I decided to tell him. He listened intently and asked a few questions. His demeanor changed entirely. He looked to me to be angry and disturbed. When I finished my story, he told me he wished I had come to him when I was a student. He said he would have removed the priest immediately.

Father Hesburgh got off the train in Baltimore. He reached above me for his travel bag, shook my hand and started to walk down the aisle. About halfway off the train, he turned and walked back to me. He said "If no one has said it to you, I apologize for what happened to you." No one had ever said that to me. To this day, he remains the only priest who has said it. It meant more to me than he will ever know.

Grandfather Tormented Us

Mike, as told to Kim Etherington

Mike was abused by his grandfather. In this selection he gives an account of the anguish the abuse caused, and the disheartening feeling of being an accomplice, rather than a victim. The essay explores the emotional tragedy of abuse, and how his grandfather stunted the personal growth of both Mike and his brother Stephen. Only after Mike breaks the silence about his grandfather's crimes, do the brothers have a chance of working through their family's baggage. The real names have been changed to protect Mike's and Stephen's identities.

I am 18 years old, an awkward and diffident boy, despite my height and beard. I find myself about to go to medical school, and I am scared. In the early 1970s it is still not so commonplace for someone of my background to go away to university. I'm not sure I shall cope. There is however at least one thing that pushes me on; for I see this move—away from home, away from town, away from the world I know—as a golden opportunity to rid myself of a dreadful obsession.

This obsession is buried deep, deep inside me. I absolutely refuse to visit it voluntarily, to contemplate it, to think of it at all; the shame and self-hate are too much. Yet it still rises unbidden from the depths to overwhelm and choke my will; and when it does I am consumed with urgent need to seek out my long time and very secret paramour, to have sex with him. He is a lot older than I am, he is my grandfather, and yet these are facts which are somehow unimportant or irrelevant to me at the time. All that I see, as I sicken with myself on the way home, is that my sin is twofold—to have sex, and to have sex with a man!

Now, as I walk through the wet dark streets, I make a decision. It will never happen again. This is a decision I have made many times before, but this time it is of a different quality: I am 18; the world sees me, or claims to see me, as an adult; I am moving away. This time I will succeed.

A New Beginning

I did succeed; I never ever had sex with him again. University life was uncomfortable, I was shy and isolated, I found few friends and all of them were women. I hovered about the other men, rather in awe, but finding no companionship— they seemed so much more adult than me. Uncomfortable it may have been, but I had managed to leave him behind.

I found an anonymous little church, approached the priest, and went to confession; I said the words, though I remember my knees nearly buckling under me, speaking and understanding only that I myself had done wrong! It seemed like the hardest thing I had ever done, but afterwards the sense of liberation was enormous. I could put down my sin and get on with my life. Here was my new start.

And so it was. I lived my new life, I achieved a degree, I started work and complained how medicine seemed to take over our lives. The medical 'system' was, I now realise, very abusive, but I wouldn't have put it that way, and of course I was ripe to be used! However I survived, when some didn't; I succeeded in my profession. I rarely thought about my childhood. I wondered vaguely if I was homosexual but as I was so awkward in the company of men I did not see how this could be put into practice! I was very lonely, I used to imagine that one day I would have a warm and loving family of my own; I remember that it was very important to me that this warmth and love would be accessible to others, that it should and could be shared. How I was to move from my loneliness to this idyllic scene was a bit of a blur!

Finding Love

I had proposed to a girl from home whilst still a student, but then I had broken it off, telling her that I had had a homosexual past relationship. Ironically, at the time this felt like an excuse. My 'real' reasons for breaking it off seemed to be many, and largely to do with the fact that she didn't fit in with the social expectations of others. My parents certainly didn't approve! I would not admit to myself my fear, and I saw no connection between this confused attempt at a relationship and my past. She came out of it with dignity, and perhaps a lucky escape!

After I had been working for a year or so, I met and was amazed to fall in love with my wife. She was pretty and vivacious, outgoing and demonstrative, tough and prickly, the life and soul of the party; my complete opposite. I loved to please her, to do whatever she asked of me. This time I made sure that, when things began to get serious, I told her about my previous 'sexual relationship with a man'. To my great joy it seemed unimportant to her; to my even greater joy she agreed to marry me. Within six months we were married with great celebration. Yes, surely I had put down my past: God had forgiven me, and it seemed irrelevant to my wife.

Revisiting the Past

Now I was surely not unintelligent, but nevertheless I did not see what happened to me in any other terms than those I have described. My sexual past had never seemed other than something for which I was responsible; even if, to my shame, I had been unable to control it. I do not believe that memory of my experiences was ever truly unavailable to me, even the fact that the beginning of my abuse was shrouded in mist somewhere in my very early childhood. I simply had no other terms of reference with which to think about it. The sexual abuse of children in general, and my own in particular, was something I simply did not think about.

This surely was not only personal, but also societal. Even professionally, in those days, it was rarely discussed. We were taught to look out for children being physically abused (euphemistically referred to as non-accidental injury); we heard mention of sexual abuse of little girls by men, but the fact that those little girls became women with problems was ignored. The fact that boys could be victims, let alone grow into adults having to cope with their past, was unthought and unspoken. No wonder I felt alone.

Becoming a Father

I first realised that what had happened to me was sexual abuse in my early thirties. Our daughter was nearly six and my wife was expecting our son. It was an explosive experience! As I write this I remember vividly the hot sensation that flooded over me as the truth dawned. I do not remember why or how the realisation came to me. I do remember wondering what to do with it. The difficulties in our marriage were bad enough to be hard to ignore. I felt that my childhood was implicated and that I should probably be asking for help. But from whom and from where? The only source of help I could think of was psychiatry, and that idea was instantly placed as a very last resort indeed! I could not imagine any of the psychiatrists with whom I had worked or whom I knew being able to help. After all, I had never come across such a situation in my time working in psychiatry! So as there was no help to be had, I should just get on with my life as I had before. I had lived with my past when I felt it to be my responsibility, surely it would be easier now that I had recognised it for what it was.

However, the cork was now working loose in the bottle. My wife, a gregarious person and always happy to make a large family occasion, had invited my parents and my grandfather, despite my reluctance, to spend a few days with us over Christmas. I had assumed that I would be able to endure this, as I had on so many other occasions in the past. But, at that time I had not seen the connection, but now I found myself saying to her, 'I have something to tell you; I think I was sexually abused as a child.' All that I remember of her reaction was that it was very angry, and that she was insistent about knowing who had done this to me, and what precisely. The cork seemed to be slipping faster; I could see that now I had shared this knowledge with another, I had lost control of it. This is a truly terrifying experience.

Eventually I did tell her, and of course her immediate reaction was to insist that he must not come for Christmas, and that if I did not stop him, then she would tell my parents in order to prevent the visit. Panic! Events out of my control!

Confronting the Abuser

And so came my epic journey on a dark and wet autumn evening to confront him. Simply put, I told him that I now realised that he had sexually abused me; that my wife knew; that he had wrecked my life; that he was not to come to our house ever again; and that if he did not pull out of the Christmas visit, we would tell my parents.

As I was talking to him it came to me that once when we were children, my younger brother had told me about 'what Grampy does in bed'. I told him that I suspected that he had abused my brother too and that I wondered how many more of our cousins he might have treated in the same way. He denied any of the others, and then said he had only done what he had done to me because I enjoyed it! I remember forcing myself to say, but wondering whether it held conviction, 'But I was a child'. In the end he accepted that he had done wrong and asked me to forgive him. I told him that I wasn't sure that I could, and then left meekly at his bidding! I do not think I showed him any of my anger. I never saw him again.

Looking for Help

He acted swiftly, arranging to move into an old people's home, telling the family that he didn't feel safe on his own any more! His children were all puzzled by this, but the Christmas visit was off—problem solved.

I began, very surreptitiously, to scour bookshop shelves for anything that could help me understand. I quickly discovered that there were books, both academic and self-help, for practically every kind of difficulty but mine! On a trip to Oxford one day I did discover two small books for women abuse survivors. I read them avidly and secretly! It was a strange experience. So much was familiar to me that it was a great relief, but the issue was dealt with in such a feminist way; women writing to women as victims of men, in a society where women expect to be victims of men. Exciting, yet desperately depressing. What about me?

Life in general seemed to carry on much as before. Then my grandfather became ill and began to die. My father couldn't understand why I did not go to visit him and I would only say that we had fallen out. When I heard he was near death I took pity and telephoned him. I spoke perhaps only two sentences; but told him that I had been trying hard to forgive him as he had asked, and that I thought I had succeeded. He died a day or so later, off the hook. The funeral was dreadful for me. However, I really felt that my problem had been buried with him. How wrong could I have been?

No Help from Family

A few months later my parents were planning to visit us; my father told me that he had found some old home movies of my grandfather with me and the others as children and that he was planning to bring them to show us. I was mortified but said nothing at the time. However, as the days passed, I realised that I couldn't do this and that eventually I was going to have to tell them about what had happened to me from about the age of five years old.

To this day I do not know how I managed to do it, but I went to see them and could think of no way but to blurt it out, 'I don't want you to bring over the films of my grandfather.' My father said, 'OK' and seemed to shrink into his chair, but my mother asked, 'Why ever not?' So I told them, 'Because he sexually abused me from the age of about five.'

To say those words felt as if my heart was being torn from my chest. My father fled the room shouting, 'Oh no!' My mother was, at first, unbelieving. 'You must have misinterpreted.' I found myself, to my horror, explaining fairly bluntly, some of what he had done. I also told her that I thought he might have abused my brother also. Then I could stay there no longer. I simply had to leave. My mother wanted me to help them, but I was just unable to do it.

Things seemed to close down. Little more was said. I heard hints that my parents' relationship was 'in trouble', but I had too much of my own in that department to worry much for them; the unacknowledged anger in our marriage was spiralling almost beyond belief.

Reconnecting with My Brother

Now my brother and I had never really been close. I had never understood why, but was not really surprised that we had little contact. I was conscious vaguely that I was missing something that other people enjoyed in their relationships with siblings; I had buried again my suspicions about him.

Our mother, however, had not! She would drop hints from time to time that he wanted to get in touch with me, but I tried to take little notice of this. Eventually came a family invitation to tea. I desperately tried to avoid being alone with him, but eventually he cornered me in the garden and announced that Mum had spoken to him and that he thought we had something in common. Panic! We arranged to meet and discuss it.

We met and talked for hours. I remember feeling exhausted, wanting to stop for a rest, and yet being unable to stop; the pressure of words seemed to just keep coming, first from one, then the other, and yet with many pauses to check out whether what was being disclosed was not too shocking to be said.

The facts of our abuse were very similar. However, it seemed that he had been much less aware of what had happened than I had, until our mother had asked him about it. The impact on him was much more sudden and dramatic. I was unable to suggest any help other than mutual support which we had at last been able to discover in each other. I felt guilty that I had no knowledge or idea that there was anyone to turn to. I did let him have some of the 'helpful hints' that I had culled from the books I had found.

Searching for Support

Then came the news that he too had found a book in a bookshop, this one written specifically about adult male survivors of sexual abuse. I travelled in search of a copy. What a tremendous sense of relief. I cannot emphasise enough just how important it was. For someone in our position, searching for a book may be the most exposure one can risk in seeking help. I still remember vividly how risky it felt to be standing at those bookshelves, and how I travelled to other towns in order to be sufficiently anonymous.

When my brother, in the most tortuous way, discovered a therapist, I was pleased for him. He tried hard to encourage me to do the same but I still didn't see it as something that could practically be available to me. The fact was that my professional position rendered enormous difficulties for me in seeking help. Eventually he suggested that therapy with the same counsellor might be an option, and with great reluctance I took the plunge.

An Abusive Mother

Fred Mimmack

In the following text, Fred Mimmack writes about the devastating effects of mother-son incest, and how he has tried to break the taboo surrounding the topic. Growing up with a mother who was a victim of child abuse herself, Mimmack became his mother's confidante and only friend. Though outwardly successful in his profession, for years he wrestled with low self-esteem and severe challenges as a husband and father. Fred Mimmack is Clinical Professor of Psychiatry at the University of Colorado Health Sciences Center. He also teaches in the training programs of the Denver Institute for Psychoanalysis.

My name is Fred Mimmack. I am a survivor of incest from my earliest years until age 13. The incestuous relations were with my mother. The effects upon my physical and psychological development, my school and work performance, my friendships and love relationships were profound, but I didn't begin to face the facts completely until about six years ago. I have lived a life of secret shame. . . .

I am 60 years old. I am a husband, a father, and a grandfather. I am a physician. I have practiced psychiatry and psychoanalysis in Denver for over 30 years. I am respected as a clinician and as a teacher at the University of Colorado Health Sciences Center. By any reasonable standard, my life is a success. But for most of those 60 years, I have not respected myself and my achievements have felt fraudulent to me, because I have been hiding a shameful secret truth.

The Turning Point

On December 1st, 1992, Marilyn VanDerbur Atler was the speaker at Grand Rounds for the Department of Obstetrics and Gynecology at the Health Sciences Center. I had arranged

Fred Mimmack, "Mother-Son Incest," *MaleSurvivor*, September 14, 2006. Reproduced by permission of the author.

for my class of psychiatric residents to be present to hear her message. Prior to that, I had had some correspondence with her, and had heard her speak publicly on two occasions, but I was not prepared for what she did that day following her presentation. She asked survivors to stand. I stood. It took almost no thought for me to do that. It was the truth. It was a relief to say it. I am a survivor. At that moment, I felt that not to stand would have [meant] continuing to hide the truth. That was my first public disclosure. This is my second. A psychiatrist is trained not to disclose personal, private information about himself or herself. That rule, like so many rules, when incompletely understood, has been carried to ridiculous extremes. I believe that many facts are readily available and should not be denied, and other realities can be intuitively perceived, so I'm breaking the rule here tonight. In my own experience working with survivors of sexual abuse, we often get to a critical point in the therapy when he or she knows that I am a survivor, and asks. It comes through in facial expression, in the wording of a question, in a pause or hesitation, or the patient simply has the sensitivity and the intuition to know it. For me to deny it, or to say: "I wonder why you ask" is to play a cruel mind game, and we have all had too many mind games played on us. It's not only our bodies which have been violated; our minds have been violated. I hope that telling you my story tonight will resonate somehow with the work that you are doing, and encourage you in that work. . . .

My mother was an incest victim herself, and remained a victim until her death at age 74. She never healed. She was violated by her father and, I suspect, by one or more of her brothers. For the 35 years that I knew her, her life was dominated by shame, guilt, self-loathing and the hatred of men. Even on her death-bed, her last words to my father were the most bitter, hateful, cruel words imaginable, and he did not deserve that; he was not the person responsible for her abuse. Very early in my life, she established a bond with me which excluded my father and sister as much as possible. She often said that she lived vicariously through me. For her, that meant possessing my mind and body. For me, it meant being so close to her that I identified with her in every way: her shame, her guilt, her fears, her hatreds. She hated her body; I hated my body. I insisted upon covering my body from head to toe—wearing long-sleeved shirts buttoned at the neck, and long pants always. I made myself a freak and I developed no physical skills or comfort with sports. I was afraid of separation from my mother and believed that I could not survive without her. She made suicide threats and swore me to secrecy about them. Secrecy and seething rage were the undercurrents in our home. I stayed by my mother's side and listened to her endlessly. I developed phobias and panic symptoms, making me even more certain that my body was defective. My father kept his distance, and he responded with silence to my mother's contemptuous verbal attacks on him. He and I did almost nothing together, and I knew him only through her eyes. Eventually I became as skillful at verbally abusing him as she was. That seemed safer than trying to get close to him and risking my mother's disapproval.

Becoming a Man

When I was 15, my mother told me of her sexual abuse at the hands of her father, when she was a teenager and her mother was ill. Her father was a notorious womanizer who shamed his family. When my mother told me this, I had not fully repressed what had occurred between us earlier, but I had mentally split off its significance. In fact, for most of my life I have denied that what she did with me amounted to abuse or incest. It was just something that happened. She said that she was telling me of her abuse as a warning—that her father and the other men in her family were "over-sexed," and now that I was old enough to ejaculate, I would be over-sexed too. I would be a beast like all men. I was paralyzed with confusion.

I secretly longed to become manly, but this was an ugly picture of manliness. It confused me that my mother seemed so unaware that I had no sex life, that I was a sissy, a freak, a wimp. No girl was in danger of being ravished by me. I stuck to the "brainy" asexual girls in high school and if anything sexual did appear in the atmosphere, I developed panic symptoms with muscle spasms and complete anesthesia in vital parts of my body. This was the beginning of various forms of sexual dysfunction which followed me into adult life just one more proof to myself that there was something terribly wrong with me. That became my conscious secret: that I was defective and deviant; I couldn't be a man. I compensated with intellectual achievement, but I didn't value it because I felt I was hiding behind it, that I was deceiving people, and that sooner or later I would be found out. This feeling of transience and fraudulence has permeated all of my work and all of my relationships, causing me to hold back, trying to protect my self from the inevitable loss and humiliation. I went ahead and did the things "normal" people do and which I really wanted to do, but felt I was faking: I went to an excellent university and medical school, established a career, married, had children, but there was always that nagging feeling that I was a fraud and could lose it all. It saddens me terribly now to face how much of myself I have held back from the people whom I love the most. I felt like I was struggling to perform with no solid foundation, and sometimes my rage would break through. It horrifies me to recognize that rage has usually taken the same form as my mother's rage, and usually with those closest to me. I'm still working on that.

Moving Out

It's hard to say when the work of recovery started for me. Surely leaving home at 17 to go to college was critical. That must have done something toward establishing safety for me, although it took many years for me to know how to be really safe. Making it in college helped, because my mother predicted I'd be back home in a week—"too frail." Being accepted by the university itself and by new friends was healing. Even though I couldn't fully believe it, there was enough there to keep me going. Acceptance to medical school was an unbelievable thrill, although my mother eroded my joy by telling me that her brother had used his influence to get me in. I believed that for years, and felt fraudulent as usual, but there were great teachers, great classmates, and the atmosphere of passionate learning that helped chip away at the self-doubting and the old ugly self-image. Meeting, courting and marrying my wife has been a vital healing force. My mother refused to attend the wedding, and my father and sister did not have the courage to attend without her. In spite of my feeling of fraudulence, my wife has provided safety and constancy for me. She has had a solid enough sense of herself, that when I would fly into one of my self-righteous, paranoid tantrums, she would not get drawn in, would wait it out, and get on with business when it was over. That's not to say that my efforts to make her feel that she was abusing me didn't hurt, they did, but she simply knew that she wasn't abusing me, and that steady, unabashed honestly has helped me to stop blaming her and start examining myself. We're still doing some healing work. My moods and tantrums were more damaging to our sons whose developing young minds were much more vulnerable to assault. I have a great deal of healing work to do with them.

Choosing the profession of psychiatry has opened up an ideal field for my search for the truth about myself, as I searched for the truth about others. I am so grateful to my patients who have shared their lives and their courage with me. Their work of healing has furthered my own. The same is true of my students.

Recovery

I did have some formal treatment. In my 40's, I entered a personal psychoanalysis which lasted 7 years. It was helpful in relieving depressive and phobic symptoms, and in freeing up useful energy. It even saved my life, but it didn't integrate the issue of sexual abuse. It couldn't: I hid from my analyst those symptoms of which I was the most ashamed. Had I revealed them, we could have confronted the issue of incest, by integrating those symptoms with the scattered and fragmented memories that were present. That confrontation and integration has been done pretty much on my own, backed up by a great support system. I'm not sure of all the reasons for its taking so long. Perhaps one reason is that very thing: that I did try to do so much of it on my own. I know that new knowledge, published in the last several years, about incest, child abuse and sexual abuse, and clearer treatment techniques for post-traumatic stress disorder have inspired and changed me. In recent years, I've done a lot of physical training and that has done a lot to change my body image, and hence my self-image. My sons who are all very athletic have been my inspiration for that, and they have directly [influenced me] with encouragement and participation.

Facing the complete truth about myself has been painfully wrenching, but freeing and strengthening, including that day last December when I stood with other survivors. It was a symbol for facing the truth. What happened between me and my mother is the truth. The way in which it crippled me is the truth. The distorted means I developed for hiding and yet expressing my bitterness and rage are the truth; but the good in me is also the truth. It's taken a long time for me to be able to say that. Recently a young woman survivor heard my story and asked me: "How could your wife live with you?" I said: "She loves me." Six or seven years ago, although I knew that, I would not have let myself say that so spontaneously. My wife always knew that I had been abused; she knew it intuitively, but she has found something in me to love, and she has provided me with safety and support.

SOCIAL ISSUES
FIRSTHAND

CHAPTER 3

The Perpetrators
of Abuse

A Victim Works with Sex Offenders

Pamela D. Schultz

In this selection therapist Pamela Schultz recounts her personal story of child abuse. Having been molested by a neighbor, the young woman struggles to acknowledge her memories and instead buries herself in academic research, drugs, and alcohol. When her work finally forces her to deal with her past, she becomes interested in the molesters' motivations. Thinking that she will be able to better accept what happened to herself if she can grasp what made her neighbor become an aggressor, she works with prison inmates and records their stories. Pamela Schultz is an associate professor in the Communication Studies program at Alfred University. She lives with her family in western New York.

L et me establish one pertinent issue at the outset: I am a survivor of child sexual abuse.

I was molested by a neighbor for years. Freed from the necessity of employment due to a mysterious chain of work-site accidents that left him on perpetual disability, The Man Who Molested Me was a fixture in our neighborhood. Since this was the 1960s and '70s, he enjoyed his status as the only man on the block during the day. After the other men left their tidy suburban tract homes early and went to work, this affable, boisterous man held court at various women's homes, drinking coffee and flirting shamelessly, always ready to lend a hand in assorted chores such as baby-sitting. He had unfettered access to any number of potential victims. I doubt I was the only child he molested. In fact, I know that I wasn't, since years later, when I began to deal with my memories of molestation, I discovered that he had victimized my sister as well.

Moving Away

He's dead now, so it doesn't cost me anything to share this information. I'm not betraying a confidence or destroying a family. No one can accuse me of being a liar. The Man Who Molested Me has been dead for twenty years. The memories of what he did, of whom he hurt, ought to be buried with him. The other children in the neighborhood, the countless kids who lived on my block in the other cookie-cutter brick homes, have long since become adults and moved away. I imagine many of us now have children of our own, and that we spend a lot of time worrying about how to protect our sons and daughters from terrorists, serial killers, and child molesters. I imagine some of us remember how it felt when we were sexually abused.

Acting Out the Trauma

I managed to disentangle myself from my abuser once I became a teenager. No doubt I became less attractive to him once I entered puberty and, as my involvement in after-school activities increased, I was able to avoid him on a regular basis. However, I ended up acting out the trauma, over and over, until my late twenties. I was a textbook example of an abuse victim. I used food and sex to sublimate my inner pain; I put a wall of fat around me to keep me safe; I approached each day as though I was on stage, carefully constructing a role to play. I did not directly confront the proverbial demon that dictated my ultimately self-destructive behavior. Somehow, I managed to function well enough to double major in college and go on to graduate school.

While I was in my first year of my master's program, The Man Who Molested Me died suddenly. My mother called to tell me the news. She seemed surprised, even saddened, when I made up a lame excuse not to drive the two hours home for the funeral. Then I proceeded to have a rather loud, swift, emotional breakdown. For a couple of months, I did a fairly good job of keeping my temporary insanity to myself, before I slipped back into the dizzying routine of studying, partying, and sleeping that defined graduate life. If I drank a bit more heavily, or began to smoke bowl after bowl of marijuana on my own, often mixing it with hashish to achieve utter numbness, no one really noticed. Most people go through some sort of emotional plunge while in graduate school. For some of us, it is a rite of passage.

Retrieving Memories

For a few more years, I was able to stave off dealing with the rotting mass of memories that clung to the back of my consciousness. If someone had outright asked if I had ever been molested, I would have quickly and sincerely answered no. I truly did not fathom that I had been sexually victimized, although of course I knew it had happened. I felt as connected to the memories of abuse as I would feel to images recalled from a disturbing film. Although I could recall the plot, and even some of the actual events, it had no emotional resonance. So it was an utter shock when, one night during the first year of my doctoral program, a wave of crystal clear memories came washing over me as I slept. I went to bed the night before never suspecting I had been molested. When I awoke the next morning, I was a victim.

My graduate stipend included insurance, so I sought out a psychiatrist. Although he didn't automatically inspire trust—he was a dark, swarthy, and energetic man who was uncomfortably reminiscent of my abuser—he was able to prescribe some excellent drugs to quiet the shrieking in my head. Then the potent mixture of tranquilizers and Halcion [a sedative] pushed me over the edge. One day I began to weep uncontrollably. When I was finally able to stop crying a week later, I realized that I wasn't going to be able to once again willfully forget what had happened. I had to figure out some way to cope with it. So I weaned myself off the medications, albeit regretfully, and focused on working out my problems through therapy.

Therapy

I don't think I was a very good patient. Despite the psychiatrist's earnest efforts to lead me along the acceptable regimen of denial/anger/grief/acceptance, I irascibly followed my own path. I tried to feel anger toward The Man Who Molested Me, but it didn't last long. Instead, I had to admit that I still loved him, not in a sexual way, but as a father figure or perhaps a valued friend, who must have been terribly wounded himself to have hurt me so badly. This attitude perplexed and eventually frustrated the psychiatrist, who seemed to feel that I had to hate The Man Who Molested Me before I could heal. I didn't know how to explain to the psychiatrist how I had become an accomplice to the crime, that The Man Who Molested Me had wheedled me into participating in my own abuse through little gifts and extravagant compliments that made the underlying threat seem bearable. By the time I had realized what was happening to me, it was too late to break free. I felt trapped, enmeshed in guilt. So I kept silent. I didn't tell anyone what was happening to me because I thought it was my fault. I wanted to protect my parents from knowing what a terrible child I was.

The psychiatrist also couldn't accept the lack of animosity toward my parents, who for years hadn't recognized their daughter's suffering. Yet why would they ever suspect the helpful, friendly, funny next-door neighbor of such heinous behavior? In the '60s and '70s, an aura of innocence still surrounded suburban life. Sexual abuse was hardly the trendy household phrase it has since become. Parents dutifully warned their children not to talk to strangers, but they never specified what those dangerous strangers might actually do.

How could my parents suspect their friend of a crime that, at the time, was nearly inconceivable?

Hurting Myself

Despite the psychiatrist's ultimately unsuccessful struggle to squeeze me into an acceptable semblance of a sexual abuse victim, he did help me make some tough realizations about my life to that point. I knew I had tried to kill myself in the past, although I never consciously defined it as such. I was frequently compelled to test fate by driving my car recklessly, drinking and smoking too much, sleeping with men I barely knew, experimenting with marijuana, cocaine, amphetamines, whatever drug was available at the time. Experiencing a slight headache, I'd swallow two aspirin, then four, then nine or ten, and wait with detached interest for whatever would result. I had always suffered bouts of low self-esteem, feeling uncomfortable in my flesh, hating the way I looked. Sometimes, I would dig at my arms or my thighs with a safety pin, a thumbtack, or even a pen cap. Watching the blood well up felt good, somehow, because the wound was something I made myself and could control. I had to admit that I had spent the greater part of my life running and hiding—from my family, from people who could hurt me, from myself. I thought I knew who I was, but suddenly I had to accept the wrenching realization that everything inside me existed because of—or in spite of—my childhood victimization.

Searching for Reasons

Unwilling to dig too far into the emotional ramifications of my abuse, I did the next best thing: I intellectualized it. I devoured books on child sexual abuse, even turned class projects into a chance to further explore the issue. I desperately wanted to understand why this man had used me. I felt that if I could comprehend the motivations behind molesting a child, I could come to terms with the ambiguous feelings that haunted me concerning my own abuse. While I researched the subject, I kept regular sessions with the psychiatrist. This went on for almost two years, then the psychiatrist said something disturbing that made me leave and never return. Almost casually, one day he told me, "The issue is not how an adult male can be turned on by a little girl. Little girls can be sexually provocative, and any healthy man can become aroused. The issue is whether the man follows through on those feelings. There's a fine line between feelings and actions."

I couldn't accept this. How could children be sexually provocative? As a woman, I had certainly never been sexually aroused by a young boy, so why would I believe all men were sexually aroused by little girls? The image was more than disgusting—it was absurd. And yet, from all the reading I had done up to this point, I knew that child sexual abuse was hardly an isolated phenomenon, nor something new to modern society. All that has changed is our willingness to acknowledge it. The psychiatrist's comment fed my need to understand why an adult could be sexually attracted to a child. I had to know why, how, what it all meant to me and to the countless other victims struggling to overcome their childhood degradation.[. . .]

Going Public

I completed my dissertation in the fall of 1994. At that time, New York was considering adopting its own version of Megan's Law [laws that require the registration of sex offenders]. Although the idea of having policies informing people of convicted perpetrators living in their neighborhoods ought to have comforted me as a survivor of sexual abuse, it didn't. In fact, the more I thought about the implications, the more uncomfortable I became. I decided to add my voice to the din. On November 13, 1994, the *Rochester Democrat & Chronicle* published my opinion piece, titled "New Law Won't Stop Sex Offenders." I wrote:

As a survivor of sexual abuse, I am intimately acquainted with its horrors, yet I cannot believe that convicted molesters are beyond redemption. Society's attitude that child molesters cannot be reformed simply strengthens an abuser's conviction that he will never be able to control his impulse to molest. If society holds no hope for a molester's redemption, how can he learn to trust himself?

My column inspired some dissent. The newspaper printed a few of the more interesting letters people wrote in response. Some were politely indignant (albeit sympathetic to my admission of victimization), and a few were downright strident, even accusing me of being an advocate for pedophiles. Mostly, my views were received with bemused disbelief. How could a victim speak out for the offenders? Was she brainwashed, or just plain deluded? At the time, I wasn't completely certain myself. I was still struggling with a deep-seated need to understand the motivations of The Man Who Molested Me. I knew he had loved me, in his own way. I wanted to believe he would have felt guilty about his actions and would have tried to make amends, if only someone had intervened. I wanted to believe that I was more than just a convenient vessel.

Visiting a Prison

As a result of the article, I received a telephone call from one of the counselors at a nearby correctional facility. He told me about the sex offender program they had begun in the prison, and he invited me out for a visit. On a gray December morning, I headed out to the facility. When I pulled my car into the visitor's parking lot, I noticed uneasily that the tall fences surrounding the prison were topped with barbed wire. When I rang at the gates, the guard buzzed me in, and then the door banged shut behind me. For a split second, I felt an impulse to flee. I focused on the fact that I had become a very public survivor of sexual abuse, and that none of the men I'd be meeting had any control over me. They couldn't—I was no longer that helpless little victim who kept blindly reacting to her abuse, over and over again. At the end of the day, I'd be able to leave the fences and barbed wire and guards behind. I was free—in every sense of the word. I wasn't letting my abuser dictate my life anymore.

Wanted to Know Why

An hour later, I was shut in a small, stuffy room with a couple of counselors and an astonishing variety of sex offenders. Ranging from exhibitionists to aggressive rapists, they all had one thing in common: they looked so normal. Some peeked at me nervously as they haltingly described their crimes. A few tried to stare me down. "Why are you here?" one man asked bluntly. I had to think about that one before finally admitting that I was simply curious. I told them that I wanted to get to know them, to try to understand why they hurt people. I wanted to know what pain in their lives had made them capable of inflicting such degradation on other people.

They all knew I had been molested. The counselor who called me had made copies of the newspaper article and passed them around. If I expected that this knowledge might give the offenders power over me, I was wrong. It actually had the opposite effect. They were curious, too, and they were grateful that I was willing to speak candidly to them about my experience. In their self-help group, they were being taught how to show empathy. They wanted to know what it was like to be a victim; they wanted to know what their own victims must have felt. So after the initial awkward silence, their questions spilled out like a flood. At the end of the two-hour session, I felt drained, but in a sort of buoyant, giddy way. It was a catharsis to sit in that close, dank room and share the impact of my abuse with men who might have done the same things to similar little girls and women. I even felt like I might have left a lingering impression on a few of them.

A Chance for Redemption

Although I had publicly pontificated on the need to help offenders find treatment rather than indiscriminately punishing them, I hadn't really thought through the implications to that point. Seeing this group in action, talking to the counselors who were spending long, emotionally exhausting hours to make their treatment program work, made me realize that perhaps there was some hope for their redemption. When the counselors I met with told me I should consider putting together a research plan and working with their inmates, it seemed only logical. Ever since I had begun my recovery, ever since my own victimization, I had moved toward this opportunity. Yet before I embarked upon this research, which entailed spending hours alone with individual offenders with nothing but a tape recorder between us, I had to wrestle with my motives. Why was I compelled to do this? Did I view studying child molesters as a form of self-therapy? Was I too subjective, did I have too many expectations, would my bias twist whatever I might discover? Was I simply masochistic?

Not Monsters

The answers to these questions became irrelevant as the interviews unfolded. The men who have spoken to me are not monsters, however monstrous the crimes they committed. They all have their own stories, with unique sets of circumstances that led to their crimes, yet there are many similarities as well. Identifying these patterns can give us glimmers of why people molest children and how we should treat offenders to keep them from repeating their crimes. Most importantly, listening to these stories can show what steps we need to take to prevent children from falling victim to these predators.

Spending time with these men has taught me a lot, not only about them, but about The Man who Molested Me. Oddly enough, the more I've come to understand his weakness, lack of character, and warped value system that gave him permission to molest me, the easier it's been to forgive him. I know now that he was trapped in his own web of deceit and inner angst, woven from a pattern that was probably passed down from generation to generation. There's no excuse for what he did to me, but there were reasons for it. Understanding the reasons has given me a measure of peace.

A Cycle of Abuse

Billy, as told to Pamela D. Schultz

Billy was repeatedly abused as a child and early on learned to use violence in order to get what he wanted from women. In this testimony, he recounts a life of brutality, secret rapes of young girls, and finally his trial and imprisonment. After years of denial, he made the decision to take responsibility for what he did. Talking about his years as a child molester, he tries to understand his own actions and find a way out of his destructive behavior. His true identity is not disclosed.

When I was young, my dad kept moving from place to place. He left us when I was six years old. He got a job driving a truck for some milk company and told my mom and us that he wouldn't be back. I more or less decided that I was going to be a tough guy after that. I was the second oldest—I have one sister older than me and a younger brother and sister—and I always stuck up for my brothers and sisters. I was the troublemaker in the family.

Before my dad left and [when] I was a real little kid, we had an old white-faced Hereford bull. When my dad would go to work in the morning, he'd take me with him and sit me on the back of this bull, and we'd just ride around the pasture all day. So instead of a little kid having a dog for a pet, I had this big old two-ton bull. I still got a picture of it. He ended up hamburger, though. I wouldn't eat none of it, either. After that, I was always bringing home cats and dogs, whatever animal I found. I used to get in trouble for it. My folks told me we ain't no dog pound. But I was always taking off and picking up strays, so they decided to start tying me to the porch. I was just three or four years old. I remember how pissed off I was because I couldn't get loose. I loved to roam around. I was always getting into stuff.

Grandfather Tried to Help

I used to run over to my grandpa's house a lot. He lived up the road. Me and my grandpa was always real close, even up to the day he died. Later on, my grandpa tried to take us kids from my mom because my stepfather was so mean, but the courts said nope. So he told my real dad what was going on, but for some reason the courts wouldn't let him have us, either. I have a lot of good memories of my grandpa. Then he had cancer, but the only thing that killed him was when they took away his beer. They took away his beer and cigars, and two months after that, he died.

My stepfather was an idiot and a drinker. If you didn't do something the way it should have been done, you got throwed around the room. He would hold your hand up and burn your fingers with a cigarette lighter. And if you decided to do something like steal, then your fingers got smashed. He mostly did it to my mom and me. I took the part, if you're going to hit somebody, hit me. That way, my brother and sisters didn't get it.

A Terrible Fight

My mother never stuck up for me with my stepfather. I guess she loved him. That was my interpretation. My one uncle that I lived with for quite a while, he was going to do something about it, but my mom told him not to. I got that scar there from my stepfather, and that's where I got my broken nose. He told me to clean the dishes one night, and instead of walking around the table to pick up a glass, I just reached across the table for it. He said to put it down and walk around there. I took the glass and slammed it down on the table, and it went all over. So we had a fight. I was twelve or thirteen and I was having none of him. He went to hit me, but I was a little too quick and took off. When I figured he was gone for the night, I came back home. It was two o'clock in the morning, but he was still there. That's how I got the broken nose, the busted eye. My mom didn't do nothing about it.

When I got up off the floor, I took off again. I was gone for three days. I had two black eyes and my nose was bleeding all over. I stayed in the woods for a while and then hung out by the laundromat. If I got thirsty, I'd go into some farmland and grab a cow's tit so I had my milk, and I'd steal donuts from behind the grocery store. But I got tired of being by myself. I finally made a collect call from the laundromat to my uncle and told him I was hiding there. What a mistake that was. He made me go back home. Back then, in order to get the cops to do something, there had to be a dead body. There was no such thing as domestic quarrels, and nobody wanted to get involved.

Molesting Other Kids

Soon after, I got in trouble all over again. This time, I got in trouble with my aunt. She was living with us at the time, and in the morning when you'd go out through the living room, she'd always be laying on the couch. That's when I started learning about sex. I just went over one day and started playing with her. I went right down to her vagina and she goes, "What are you doing?" "Looking for a yo-yo," I said. I don't know why I said that. She started laughing and made me quit, and I think that if I had gotten yelled at right then and there, I wouldn't be here now. That's just what I'm thinking. If they had put me in a home or something when I started to become a problem to everybody, maybe I'd have straightened out.

Of course, I had been about five years old when I first had sex. It was with my cousin underneath the old horse barn. She showed me what to do. She was only about five—about the same age as me—but she still knew about sex. Years later, I found out my uncle had molested all my cousins. After my cousin and I did it, there was a neighbor girl. We were like seven or eight years old and did everything, except I could never figure out how to get my penis into her so I always used my fingers. And then, later on, the incident with my aunt happened. After that, I just kept on messing around with all my cousins and the neighbor girls. I figured if they ain't yelling, then it must be all right. I've taken all these courses while I've been in prison and they keep telling me that those girls didn't want it, but none of those girls hollered like it was bothering them. I know it was wrong because I was older than them, but they didn't fight me about it.

A Bad Marriage

This went on for a long time, until I was just turned twenty and got married to my first wife. Then I just wasn't interested in sex no more. I tried to get it from my wife, but that was fighting a losing battle. All the time we was married, I think we only slept together maybe eight times. I tried to have sex with her before we got married, but it didn't work. I think that was why I married her—to say at least I finally got you. We had been going out for two years before we got married. I tried to get her attention for the longest time. I think it was the hard-to-get thing. I thought I was doing all the right things—you know, being polite and a gentleman. I'd get her roses and stuff. It took me two years before she finally says okay, we can get married. But the marriage didn't work too well. Even though she was my wife, she was never home. She was always out with her family and friends and whatever. That bugged me for a while—that every time I came home from work there was nobody there. I cleaned the house, I did all the laundry, I tried to make things pretty to get her attention. But I couldn't figure out what I was doing wrong. It didn't dawn on me that it was my attitude and the way I treated her like garbage. When I did come home and she was there, I'd get really jealous and hit her. Damn, I think I'd spend the next two hours trying to apologize, and I'd clean up the house again and do the dishes. She'd finally come downstairs and I'd try to make it up to her, and we'd start making out, and then she'd go, "I'm going out." That would make me mad and I'd hit her again. I'd say to her, "This ain't worth it—one of us has got to go." She says, "Well, what's in it for me?" "I don't know," I say. "Okay, then I'll stay," she says. This way at least she'd have a roof over her head.

Molesting His Niece

Around the time my marriage started to fall apart, my cousins started bringing my niece over, and for some reason, that is when I crossed the line. I don't know if it was because I was getting back at everybody or what. In my group here at the prison, the guys were all asking me why I done what I did with my niece, and I couldn't face it. So I quit going to the group. I kept thinking, damn, why am I thinking about this garbage? But finally I realized how deep this thing got with me and figured out that if I had gotten help when I first crossed the line, maybe I might not be here today. So I been trying to think why I did stuff with my niece. Maybe it was because I was angry or just horny, I don't know. I came right out and asked her, "Cindy, play with me." I just kept talking to her about it and she finally said okay.

Cindy was my cousin's daughter, the cousin I had played with when we was kids. I just had her fondle me and we kissed, but for some reason I felt guilty about it. Nothing was said about it until the next time she came over to baby-sit—my wife and me had one kid at the time and she was pregnant with our second. Anyhow, I kept saying to myself, nope, nope, don't do this, but there was something in my brain that kept saying, well, you did it once and it was all right, so go ahead. So I did. I'd play with Cindy, make her stand upside down or give me blow jobs. If I ever went some-place, she'd want to go with me, so I guess she felt okay about it. I was so angry at everything at that time. I think if I had had a gun, I'd have shot everybody in sight. I was always try-ing to do the right thing, but I couldn't stop the voice in my head that kept telling me to do it to her again. The only time me and my wife had sex was when she wanted to get preg-nant. So I don't know, I guess I just was pretty crazy.

Taking Advantage of a Child

The thing with my niece went on for like two years. Whenever she came over, it was like she knew what I wanted, you know. She'd come up to me and start grabbing, and I'd say, oh, she's ready for me, without realizing that was the picture I put in her brain. I just figured, she likes it. This is where the group showed me that I was the one who had her doing that, going along with me. She was just a little girl, and I put into her head that she should play with me and that it was all right. I never said nothing to her about not telling nobody. I just said to her the first time, it won't hurt, I promise, and I was nice to her. After that, it seemed just normal. Even I got to think-ing it was normal. Cindy didn't seem to care. When she didn't tell anybody and nobody said nothing to me about it, I fig-ured it was all right. I wasn't hurting her or being mean to her, and she was more or less making me happy because I was getting some attention. She thought I loved her. That's where I crossed the line. Instead of respecting her, I made her grown up before she really was.

Leaving Home

The day I left my wife, I came home from work and peeked into my neighbor's window and thought I saw him on the couch with her on top of him. So I ripped my coat off and came running through his back door. By that time, she was coming down from upstairs and he was laying on the couch. I decked her and left. My neighbor didn't do nothing. He was afraid of me, anyway. I told my wife, "That's it, we can't do this no more. You go your way and I'll go my way." I went to live in a small town a ways away for about six months. A friend of mine had a log cabin there, and he gave me a gun and shells. When I was hungry, I went out and shot rabbits or something and just stayed there by myself like an old hermit. I didn't have no job—just lived off the land. If I needed money, I took the animal hides down and my friend took them into town and sold them. Then he'd give me more shotgun shells. I was having a grand old time until I got homesick.

A Second Marriage

I moved back to my hometown and stayed by myself. About a year later, I met the woman who became my second wife. I was doing work on an apartment house and forty feet up in the air redoing a chimney. I wanted a cigarette, and the guy that was working with me wouldn't walk up the ladder. So I heard this woman down there getting a cigarette out of my truck. She walks all the way up the ladder to me and says here. Not bad, I thought. "Do you want to go out?" "Someday," she says. Hmm, I thought—I found another one that's hard to get. I would like it if a woman would just say yes, right then and there. Then I wouldn't have to go through all this work.

I tried to get her to go out with me for about three months. I'd see her down on the ground while I was working up on the roof. She'd be taking her kids to the school bus, and I'd be going, "Kibbles and bits, your ground is shaking." I guess I made her mad. The more I said that, the more she'd yell at me. But at least she was paying attention to me. Instead of climbing down the ladder, I had this habit of grabbing the sides and putting my feet on it and sliding down to the ground. I liked to show off for the neighbors. One day, when I was about halfway down, the ladder went thump and I fell.

Everybody comes over to ask me if I was all right. She was there, and that was when I asked her again if she wanted to go out. "When I can get a baby-sitter," she says. I pointed to a lady who was standing there and said, "You got one right there." So we started going out.

Getting to Know Each Other

Her name was Elaine. Things started off a little rocky because even though she was seeing me, when I'd go to work during the day, she'd go down the street to her boyfriend's house. I don't know why I stayed with her. But later on, I was putting up a picket fence, and she comes over and gives me a rose. "Here," she says. "What the heck do I want with a flower?" I says. "You aren't supposed to give a man a flower." "Yes, I can," she says. "Well, I'm not taking it," I told her. She put it on the dashboard of my truck. It smelled pretty. And we worked things out and were together ever since.

After I left my first wife, I didn't have no more contact with Cindy. I'd go over and see her and her family, but that was it. It was like she didn't exist for me anymore. She'd ask me if we were going somewhere or if I'd spend some time with her, and I'd say, "Not today, I'm busy." I guess she hated me for a while, especially later on after I first went to prison, but she got over it. After I came to prison, I talked to Cindy and told her that it wasn't her fault what I did. I made her into something she wasn't because my wife and I were having problems. Cindy paid attention to me, and she never told me no. I never pushed her. I think she loved me in a way. She was paying attention to me, and I was paying attention to her. But then I began to ignore her when my life got going okay again, and that really hurt her for a while.

The Daughter

Anyhow, back to Elaine. After she gave me that rose, things were going really good between us. Elaine had two kids, a little boy and a girl named Annie. When we were first going together, I did anything for those kids. I'd take them to the park and baby-sit them after I got home from work. Elaine lived next to a bar, and when she worked nights, I'd put the kids to bed and then go next door to the bar. I'd sit there and drink until it was time for Elaine to come home, and then I'd go back upstairs to wait for her. That was when things started between Annie and me. The first time Annie came into the bathroom when I was in there, I didn't know if she saw me or not. She just stood there when she realized I was in there. She was looking at me so hard, I thought, well, maybe she likes me, so I started trying to get her to have sex with me. She always said no, so I backed off.

Abusing the Girl

I didn't do anything with Annie until her mom and I had been together for five or six years. Elaine and me eventually got married, but it wasn't till after I was in the county jail, something like eight or nine years after we met. When things started with Annie, she was nine years old. I was always trying to be like a dad to her, but it was hard. She'd walk around the house and do little things that reminded me of sex. Why do little girls do that, you know? Swing their hips when they walk around and wear nightgowns or something that you can see through? It didn't dawn on me to tell Annie to go put her clothes on. I just ignored it. But really I didn't ignore it. I just let her do it because I thought, what the heck. Then one night Annie got messed up with poison ivy and her mother wouldn't touch it. So I had to be the one to put calamine lotion on Annie. I rubbed the stuff all over her body and when I got to her vagina, she didn't say no. Well, she didn't scream and yell at me, anyway, so I thought that maybe it was all right. So I tried playing with her. She got mad and said no. Then I got mad and I said, "You're going to let me do it or I'm going to beat you up." So she let me because I scared her.

Depression

For the next four months or so, things didn't go good for me and Elaine. I decided I wanted out. Every time I wanted to leave, though, I didn't have no money, so I just got to the point where I didn't care. I mean, I'm usually trying to do my best like cleaning up the house, but I just snapped. I was like an animal. If you left something lying around, I'd take it, or if you left your car unlocked, I'd get into it. I was stealing tools, food, you name it. I'd go into a store and take cigarettes right in front of the clerks. And they never said nothing to me. Damn, I thought, I'm going to keep doing this because I wasn't getting caught. I don't know if I wanted somebody to stop me or not. I figured I'd just see how far I could go. I tried to break into people's cars, but I ain't never got the hang of that, yet. I couldn't ever get the cars open. And I tried to get into pop machines, but that didn't work. I just didn't care if I lived or died. I was in one of those—what do you call them?— depression states. That's where I was.

Crossing the Line

This went on for a while, and then one day Annie made me mad as hell. I can't remember why she made me mad, but I said, "Okay, I'll fix you." I was so mad, I went out and got drunk so then I wouldn't have to worry about it. I thought when I got back home, everything would be all right. But it didn't work that way. Annie said to me, "You're not my dad and you can't tell me nothing." I told her to give me a kiss. She said, "No, I hate you." So I took all her clothes off and I slung her over the bed and I said, "Now I'm going to give you something." And that is when I sodomized her. I think I was bent out of shape because I was trying to compare Annie with Cindy. I just asked Cindy and it was always all right. But when I'd ask Annie the same thing, she was like, no, get away from me. I'd think, you know, you're supposed to say yes. I crossed the line. I made both of those girls grow up before it was their time. I guess I needed all their attention, but I went too far, especially with Annie. Annie was a good girl. But I screwed up her life.

When I was sodomizing Annie, she started crying and screaming, and I held her mouth so she couldn't make a sound. I was just being downright mean to her. I was like a great big ape. I didn't care if I was hurting her or not. But Elaine came home and caught us. I didn't see her at first, but I guess she just stood there for a minute. She says, "What are you doing?" "What do you think I'm doing?" I say back. I didn't care if she saw me or not. That should have clicked right there, you know. Hey, there's somebody watching. But it didn't click. I was just like a great big animal. Afterwards, I felt relieved a little bit because I had let all the anger out. I didn't think nothing about Annie. I didn't care about her. I didn't feel sorry for her. It had nothing to do with sex or love. It was just like, all right, you got the hole and I'm taking it. Annie just stood there. She wasn't crying and she didn't look like she was in pain, but if she had a gun, I'd be dead. Maybe she should have had a gun. Elaine asked her if that was the first time it happened, and she said yes. I had always been trying to grab Annie's butt or pinch her boobs, but she never said anything about that. Elaine told me she was going to call the cops. I yanked the phone off the wall and said, "I'm not going to do it again." She said okay.

Going to Prison

For the next month, it was like everything got back to normal. I thought, wow, this is decent. I never tried to play with Annie or grab her. I was more or less finally becoming a grown-up. Annie's attitude toward me was like, don't come near me, but I'll still talk to you. I helped her with her homework and I helped her with the dishes. For about a month, we were a regular family. There was no fighting, no quarrels. But Elaine told her friend Linda about what happened, and Linda didn't like me because I cracked her husband one night. So Linda called the cops and they came to get me. The cops asked me if I knew why they was there. I said, "Yeah." "Why?" "Because I sodomized my stepdaughter." I decided then that if I can go off the wall and do that to somebody without caring, then there is something really wrong with me. I was charged with sodomy first and endangering the welfare of a minor. I admitted to all of it, all but the sodomy part, that is. So we went to trial, and I was so mad and bent out of shape that I told the judge, the lawyer, the DA [district attorney], and the jury to kiss my ass and go to hell. I just didn't care.

Just before I was sentenced, Elaine came up to me and goes, "Are we still getting married?" Now, why is she asking me this after what I just did? But everybody was saying to go for the trailer visits, so I said, "Yeah, let's get married." Elaine was standing by me. I didn't have the common sense to know that even though I hurt her and her daughter, she was trying to make amends. "Why don't you go find somebody better than me?" I'd say. But she didn't want nobody but me. When I first got to prison, they said, "Well, what do you want?" I said, "I need help and I want to work in the shop." So I was making money. I'd send Elaine half and I'd keep half. It was pretty decent for a while. She'd come to visit me every weekend and bring her son, and once she brought my real boys from my first marriage. I was still on okay terms with my first wife for a long time. Even though she hated the hell I put her through, we kept talking for a while. But I haven't talked to her or my boys for the past four years. I sent the boys each a birthday card, and she sent them back, stating that I hope you appreciate my feelings and don't contact us again. So I wrote her a letter back saying that's fine, when the boys turn of age if they want to see me they know where I'm at. And that's where I left it. You know, I just don't need any of it. I got to get myself straightened out before I can think about any of those people.

Life in Prison Takes a Toll

Once, Elaine brought Annie to see me. That was an all right visit, but I felt awkward after the way I treated her. Now I was supposed to expect her to be nice to me. It don't work that way. Annie had to testify at my trial. Everybody said to take the cop-out, but I said no, I did this, and we'll go to trial so everybody will know. It was hard for Annie to testify, but she had to do it. At least her and I could talk civil to each other. But then there came a time when I wasn't getting no letters, no visits. Every time I tried to call Elaine, I'd get the answering machine. It made me nuts. Finally, she came up to see me. She goes, "I got something to tell you." I said, "What, you're pregnant?" "How do you know?" she asks. Because it wasn't hard to see—I mean, she was sticking out to there. She told me she didn't like the father and wanted to give the baby my name. I couldn't believe it. Now she's had the baby and is with another guy. I wrote to her and told her that it seemed to me she was happy and that was fine. I wish you all the love in the world, but I got to move on. So if you want a divorce, let me know and I'll be glad to give it to you. That was twelve months ago, and I still ain't heard no answer.

I was in prison for six years and four months before I really started to deal with what I done. I never even started touching any of this until two weeks before my first parole board, when I got sick. I was working up in the welding shop as a teacher's aide. I took a coat hanger and was trying to get some grease up off the floor when there was an accident. I woke up two days later and my neck was out to there—I couldn't talk and I couldn't eat. So I went to the hospital and they said I burned the glands on each side of my throat. That's when I had all these flashes and I said to myself, you've screwed up enough, now start helping people. But before you help people, you got to help yourself. And when I went to the parole board and I said, "I don't care if you believe me or not, but I'm not ready to go home," this one lady says, "You have no idea what you've done?" "No, ma'am," I said, "but I'm going to start really working on it." I told her I planned to face up to who I am and what I am.

Therapy Sessions

People said you couldn't play games in groups, but I did. I did it for six years and four months, until I got sick and made my realization. The counselors would ask me questions like, "Well, how did you get your stepdaughter to go along with you?" And I'd say, "I told her to do it, or I'd beat the shit out of her." That's all I'd say. I'd shock them, and then they'd back off. Or I'd just sit there and say, "I don't care if you don't like what I'm saying or not—that's just the way I am." And that has been me all my life. If I come out with something negative, I know I'm going to keep you way out there. I don't know why I don't want people to get close to me. I think it might be because whenever I've loved something or somebody, it's either died or taken off. Instead of me going through that hurt again, I can just keep you away from me. I think that is why I took those two little girls and made them bigger before their time—because somehow they got to me. They got too close. I didn't think of them as little girls. I made them grown up, but they weren't grown up—only in my mind. And now those two are going to go through the rest of their lives wondering if it was their fault. They might think, what is my boyfriend going to be like? What is my husband going to be like? Is he going to hurt me like Billy did? I chewed up a lot of lives.

This last group I been in here, I screwed up and left. I was getting aggravated because I wasn't ready to share anything about myself. The more aggravated I got, the more I was swearing and cussing and stuff. I figured, well, instead of getting so aggravated, I'm just going to quit. I ain't going to go. But then I got this counselor who changed me around. He is one of the few people that for some reason has gotten past that barrier I put up. I lied to him over and over, but he didn't do nothing. He just kept talking to me, and somehow he got me to trust him. I've done everything in my power to get that man to hate me, but he's still coming back. Now, even though he is a counselor here in prison and I could hate him for that, if I ever had to watch his back and give my life for him, I would do it. So now I'm trying to get back into that group, as soon as I come to grips with myself and stop playing games. I owe all the guys an apology for the way I treated them.

Not Ready to Face a Normal Life

I know I'm not ready to go home. I don't think I'll be ready to go home, even in another two more years, because I've got thirty-six years to make up for. And I could take another forty just trying to figure out who I am. So I'm trying to take that first step. You have to want to be helped. If you say that you don't have a problem, then nothing in the world is going to help you. The only thing that made me wake up was when I got so sick. I don't know if the man upstairs is looking out for me, but he seems to be doing pretty good. So I'm working on myself. Since I've been in prison, I've gotten my GED [general equivalency diploma], and I've been certified as a welder. I've become more of a man here than I ever was on the streets. I'm sorry for what I did, but I'm not sorry for coming to prison, because I've done quite a bit since I've been here. And I'm not ready to leave yet. I want to keep learning while I'm here. If I can pick up what they're trying to teach me, learn how to revamp my thinking, then it'll keep me out of trouble.

The other thing I got to work on is not to masturbate. I used to do that a lot. There was no problem with me masturbating twenty times a day. The one thing I've realized is that even though you've got the thoughts, you can change them. That's the big thing my last group taught me—how to think different. After the thing with Cindy, I used to just sit there and look at pictures of Cindy and masturbate. Same thing with my stepdaughter. Other than that, little girls didn't bother me. Most guys, they go out after many little kids, but for me it was just Cindy and Annie. Maybe it was because I really loved them as girlfriends or whatever.

Working for Redemption

I'm working on breaking down that barrier I got around me. I'm trying not to be such a tough guy. Even when I was a kid, I never let nobody see me cry, because if you cry, you are not a man. I got some screwed-up lessons when I was a kid. I should have been sent to prison long ago. When I do get out, I'm going to start going to churches and schools and tell them like it is. I got a dream that I tell the little kids that it's all right to tell somebody. If it will help get guys from hurting any more of you kids, then go ahead and say something, because it's only going to help you and it's only going to help us. It took me a long time to come to this way of thinking.

About this sex offender notification stuff—I think it is a good thing. If I get out and I'm trying to hide who I am, what's to say that I am not going to do this to some other little girl. If people know who I am and what I used to be, then they are helping me because now they are going to put their kids in check. Before, if a sex offender got out, nobody knew it. The minute he got out, he could go around the corner and do it again, because there were no programs to help him. We need programs to help us and for communities to be aware of the problem. We need that help and support, because if we don't get it, we are just going to keep doing it. Sure, I'm afraid that some people might come after me, but on the other hand, if I'm not hiding something, maybe they will leave me alone.

To keep from ever doing this again, I got to take one day at a time and keep talking. If I can keep my frustration down and not let myself get so hot-headed and angry all the time, then I can make it. I still got this little bit of the male macho-ness, you know, but I'm getting rid of it as much as I can. Now that I do have the help and the counseling, I'm going to take advantage of it. I should have been in prison a long time ago, but now I've changed my life around.

Organizations to Contact

The editors have compiled the following list of organizations concerned with the issues debated in this book. The descriptions are derived from materials provided by the organizations. All have publications or information available for interested readers. The list was compiled on the date of publication of the present volume; the information provided here may change. Be aware that many organizations take several weeks or longer to respond to inquiries, so allow as much time as possible.

Administration for Children and Families (ACF)
370 L'Enfant Promenade SW, Washington, DC   20201
Web site: www.acf.hhs.gov

The Administration for Children and Families (ACF), within the Department of Health and Human Services (HHS), is responsible for federal programs that promote the economic and social well-being of families, children, individuals, and communities.

ACT for Kids
210 West Sprague Ave., Spokane, WA   99201
(866) 348-KIDS (5437) • fax: (509) 747-0609
e-mail: info@actforkids.org
Web site: www.actforkids.org

ACT for Kids is a nonprofit organization that provides resources, consultation, research, and training for the prevention and treatment of child abuse and sexual violence. The organization publishes workbooks, manuals, and books such as *My Very Own Book About Me* and *How to Survive the Sexual Abuse of Your Child*.

Child Abuse Prevention Association (CAPA)
503 E. 23rd St., Independence, MO   64055
(816) 252-8388 • fax: (816) 252-1337

e-mail: capa@childabuseprevention.org
Web site: www.childabuseprevention.org

CAPA helps children and their families overcome the traumatic effects of child abuse, especially regarding child molestation. CAPA also provides educational programs designed to increase awareness of abuse and how to prevent it as well as providing case management and other support services to help create strong families and decrease the chances of abuse and neglect.

Child Molestation Research & Prevention Institute (CRMPI)
PO Box 7593, Atlanta, GA   30357
(404) 872-5152
e-mail: contact@childmolestationprevention.org
Web site: www.childmolestationprevention.org

The CRMPI is a national science-based nonprofit organization dedicated to preventing child sexual abuse through research, education, and family support. Because people who develop a sexual interest in children usually develop it during their teenage years and even younger, the focus is on providing information to professionals and to families about the early warning signs of a problem, as well as the availability of early diagnosis and effective treatment from a sex-specific specialist.

Child Welfare Information Gateway
1250 Maryland Ave. SW, Eighth Floor
Washington, DC   20024
(800) 394-3366
e-mail: info@childwelfare.gov
Web site: www.childwelfare.gov/index.cfm

Child Welfare Information Gateway promotes the safety, permanency, and well-being of children and families by connecting child welfare, adoption, and related professionals as well as concerned citizens to timely, essential information. The agency provides access to print and electronic publications, Web sites, and online databases covering a wide range of topics from prevention to permanency, including child welfare, child abuse and neglect, adoption, and search and reunion.

False Memory Syndrome Foundation
1955 Locust St., Philadelphia, PA   19103
(215) 940-1040 • fax: (215) 940-1042
e-mail: mail@fmsfonline.org
Web site: www.fmsfonline.org

The foundation believes that many "delayed memories" of sexual abuse are the result of false memory syndrome (FMS). In FMS, patients in therapy "recall" childhood abuse that never occurred. The foundation seeks to discover reasons for the spread of FMS, works for the prevention of new cases, and aids FMS victims, including those falsely accused of abuse. The foundation publishes a newsletter and various papers, and distributes articles and information on FMS.

National Center for Missing & Exploited Children (NCMEC)
Charles B. Wang International Children's Building
Alexandria, VA   22314-3175
(703) 274-3900 • fax (703) 274-2200
Web site: www.missingkids.com

NCMEC serves as a clearinghouse of information on missing and exploited children and coordinates child protection efforts with the private sector. A number of publications on these issues are available, including guidelines for parents whose children are testifying in court, help for abused children, and booklets such as *Children Traumatized in Sex Rings* and *Child Molesters: A Behavioral Analysis*.

Pan American Health Organization (PAHO)/
World Health Organization (WHO)
Regional Office for the Americas, Washington, DC   20037
(202) 974-3000 • fax: (202) 974 3663
e-mail: postmaster@paho.org
Web site: www.paho.org

The Pan American Health Organization is an international public health organization working to improve health and living standards in countries of the Americas. PAHO is a division of the World Health Organization, the United Nations specialized agency for health. The PAHO Web site offers information on child abuse in the Americas, including the Power-Point presentation "Child Abuse in Latin America and the Caribbean" and articles such as "A Childhood Stolen, A Society in Fear."

Prevent Child Abuse America (PCA America)
500 N. Michigan Ave., Suite 200, Chicago, IL   60611
(312) 663-3520 • fax: (312) 939-8962
e-mail: mailbox@preventchildabuse.org
Web site: www.preventchildabuse.org

Since 1972, PCA America has worked on building awareness, providing education, and inspiring hope to everyone involved in the effort to prevent the abuse and neglect of children. The organization provides leadership to promote and implement prevention efforts at both the national and local levels.

For Further Research

Books

Elizabeth Bartholet, *Nobody's Children: Abuse and Neglect, Foster Drift, and the Adoption Alternative*. Boston: Beacon Press, 2000.

John Briere, Lucy/Berliner, and Josephine A. Bulkley, eds., *The APSAC Handbook on Child Maltreatment*. Thousand Oaks, CA: Sage, 2000.

Kathleen Coulborn Faller, *Interviewing Children About Sexual Abuse: Controversies and Best Practice*. New York: Oxford University Press, 2007.

Cynthia Crosson-Tower, *Understanding Child Abuse and Neglect*. Boston: Pearson/A&B, 2005.

Nancy Davis, *Therapeutic Stories To Heal Abused Children*. Oxon Hill, MD: Psychological Associates of Oxon Hill, 1990.

Byrgen Finkelman, *Child Abuse: A Multidisciplinary Survey: Physical and Emotional Abuse and Neglect*. New York: Garland, 1995.

Mary Gail Frawley-O'Dea, *Perversion of Power: Sexual Abuse in the Catholic Church*. Nashville, TN: Vanderbilt University Press, 2007.

Richard B. Gartner, *Betrayed as Boys: Psychodynamic Treatment of Sexually Abused Men*. New York: Guilford, 1999.

Neal King, *Speaking Our Truth: Voices of Courage and Healing for Male Survivors of Childhood Sexual Abuse*. Harper Perennial, 1995.

CJP Lee, *Pervasive Perversions: Paedophilia and Child Sexual Abuse in Media/Culture*. London: Free Association, 2005.

John Lee, *The Flying Boy: Healing the Wounded Man.* Deerfield Beach, FL: Health Communications, 1987.

Mike Lew, *Victims No Longer.* New York: Harper & Row, 1990.

————, *Leaping upon the Mountains: Men Proclaiming Victory over Sexual Child Abuse.* North Atlantic, 2000.

Donileen R. Loseke, Richard J. Gelles, and Mary M. Cavanaugh, eds., *Current Controversies on Family Violence.* Thousand Oaks, CA: Sage, 2005.

Richie McMullen, *Male Rape: Breaking the Silence on the Last Taboo.* London: Gay Men's Press, 1990.

Alice Miller, *The Drama of the Gifted Child: The Search for the True Self.* New York: Basic, 1981.

————, *For Your Own Good: Hidden Cruelty in Child-Rearing and the Roots of Violence.* New York: Farrar & Straus, 1983.

————, *Thou Shalt Not Be Aware: Society's Betrayal of the Child.* New York: New American Library, 1984.

Cindy L. Miller-Perrin and Robin D. Perrin, *Child Maltreatment: An Introduction.* Thousand Oaks, CA: Sage, 2007.

Walter De Milly, *In My Father's Arms: A True Story of Incest.* Madison: University of Wisconsin Press, 1999.

Neerosh Mudaly and Chris Goddard, *The Truth Is Longer Than a Lie: Children's Experiences of Abuse and Professional Interventions.* Philadelphia: Jessica Kingsley, 2006.

David Mura, *A Male Grief: Notes on Pornography and Addiction.* Minneapolis, MN: Milkweed Editions, 1987.

John E.B. Myers, *Child Protection in America: Past, Present, and Future.* New York: Oxford University Press, 2006.

Eugene Porter, *Treating the Young Male Victim of Sexual Assault: Issues and Intervention Strategies.* Syracuse, NY: Safer Society, 1986.

Richard Rose and Terry Philpot, *The Child's Own Story: Life Story Work with Traumatized Children*. Philadelphia: Jessica Kingsley, 2005.

Edward L. Rowan, *Understanding Child Sexual Abuse*. Jackson, MS: University of Mississippi Press, 2006.

Emilie Stoltzfus, *Child Welfare: State Performance on Child and Family Services Reviews*. New York: Novinka, 2006.

Periodicals

Jay Adams, "Child Abuse: The Fundamental Issue in Forensic Clinical Practice," *International Journal of Offender Therapy and Comparative Criminology*, December 2002.

Holly Marie Antal, "The Psychological and Physical Impact of Writing About Childhood Abuse," *Dissertation Abstracts International, Section B: The Sciences and Engineering*, April 2005.

Sheila Ards, "Estimating Local Child Abuse," *Evaluation Review*, October 1989.

Sandra T. Azar and Beth R. Siegel, "Behavioral Treatment of Child Abuse: A Developmental Perspective," *Behavior Modification*, July 1990.

Emma Bevan and Daryl Higgins, "Is Domestic Violence Learned? The Contribution of Five Forms of Child Maltreatment to Men's Violence and Adjustment," *Journal of Family Violence*, September 2002.

Kathleen Coulborn Faller, "Anatomical Dolls: Their Use in Assessment of Children Who May Have Been Sexually Abused." *Journal of Child Sexual Abuse*, September 2005.

Carolyn Cousins, "But the Parent Is Trying . . .: The Dilemmas Workers Face When Children Are at Risk from Parental Substance Use," *Child Abuse Prevention: National Child Protection Clearinghouse Newsletter*, Summer 2005.

Gemma L. Gladstone, Gordon B. Parker, Philip B. Mitchell, Gin S. Malhi, Kay Wilhelm, and Marie-Paule Austin, "Implications of Childhood Trauma for Depressed Women: An Analysis of Pathways from Childhood Sexual Abuse to Deliberate Self-Harm and Revictimization," *American Journal of Psychiatry*, August 2004.

Joanne M. Hall, "Core Issues for Female Child Abuse Survivors in Recovery from Substance Misuse," *Qualitative Health Research*, September 2000.

Renee M. Johnson, Jonathan B. Kotch, Diane J. Catellier, Jane R. Winsor, Vincent Dufort, Wanda Hunter, and Lisa Amaya-Jackson, "Adverse Behavioral and Emotional Outcomes From Child Abuse and Witnessed Violence," *Child Maltreatment*, August 2002.

Julia Kim-Cohen, Avshalom Caspi, Michael Rutter, Mónica Polo Tomás, and Terrie E. Moffitt, "The Caregiving Environments Provided to Children by Depressed Mothers With or Without an Antisocial History," *American Journal of Psychiatry*, June 2006.

Amy Leventhal, Teresa Jacobsen, Laura Miller, and Elena Quintana, "Caregiving Attitudes and At-Risk Maternal Behavior Among Mothers With Major Mental Illness," *Psychiatric Services*, December 2004

Brian E. Oliver, "Preventing Female-Perpetrated Sexual Abuse," *Trauma, Violence, & Abuse*, vol. 8, no. 1, 2007.

Martin H. Teicher, Jacqueline A. Samson, Ann Polcari, and Cynthia E. McGreenery, "Sticks, Stones, and Hurtful Words: Relative Effects of Various Forms of Childhood Maltreatment," *American Journal of Psychiatry*, June 2006.

Index

A

Alesandro, John, 55
Atler, Marilyn VanDerbur, 69

C

Charter for the Protection of
Children and Young People (U.S.
Conference of Catholic Bishops),
47
child abuse
account of cycle of, 86–102
body as expression of, 22
by family friends, account of,
14–17
long-term consequences of,
10–11, 56–57, 72
types of, 10
crime/delinquency, among child-
abuse victims, 11

D

Department of Health and Human Services, U.S. (HHS), 10

E

emotional abuse
by mother, account of, 26–39
as percent of total child victims, 10

H

Huneke, Robert, 49–52

M

McGann, John, 53

N

National Institute of Justice (NIJ),
11
neglect, as percent of total child
victims, 10

P

parents
abused as children, perpetua-
tion of abuse by, 12
perpetrators, 10
former victims of child abuse
as, 11–12
physical abuse
by father, account of, 18–24
as percent of total child victims, 10

R

recovery
process of, 73–74
through working with abusers, 84–85

S

self-abuse, 80
sex offenders, account of victim
working with, 76–85
sexual abuse
by father, account of, 40–46
by grandfather, account of,
61–68
by mother, account of, 69–74
as percent of total child victims, 10
by priest, account of, 47–60

T

therapy, 79–80, 99–100

U

U.S. Conference of Catholic Bishops, 47

V

victims
  drug/alcohol use by, 16, 78
  recovery and involvement in abuse intervention, 48
  self-abuse by, 80
  working with sex offenders, account of, 76–85